SELF-PUBLISH
YOUR N[OVEL]
MADE EASY

My story

Chapter One

This is a **FLAME TREE** book
First published 2014

Publisher and Creative Director: Nick Wells
Project Editors: Laura Bulbeck and Polly Prior
Art Director and Layout Design: Mike Spender
Digital Design and Production: Chris Herbert
Screenshots: Richard N. Williams
Copy Editor: Daniela Nava
Proofreader: Dawn Laker
Indexer: Helen Snaith

Special thanks to: Kamara Williams

This edition first published 2014 by
FLAME TREE PUBLISHING
Crabtree Hall, Crabtree Lane
Fulham, London SW6 6TY
United Kingdom

www.flametreepublishing.com

14 16 18 17 15
1 3 5 7 9 10 8 6 4 2

© 2014 Flame Tree Publishing

ISBN 978-1-78361-232-1

Printed in China

All non-screenshot pictures are courtesy of Shutterstock and © the following contributors: Masson 1; Denphumi 3; Olesya Feketa 9;
Goodluz 10; Pixsooz 10; Roobcio 11; Elnur 15; Phoelix 16; Andrey_Popov 18; Denniro 19; baranq 24; Rafal Olkis 26; Pressmaster 28t;
racorn 29; Christo 31t; baranq 33t; Stable 35; Yuriy Vlasenko 36; tanatat 43; Jurgita Genyte 46; MJTH 47; R Carner 50; Andresr 53;
goldyg 59t; Everett Collection 61; Ermolaev Alexander 63t; Africa Studio 69; Gts 70; Andrey_Popov 76t; Pixsooz 79b; dean bertoncelj 80;
Giakita 84; Catherine Murray 86; Mila Supinskaya 92t; Ermolaev Alexander 93; Gst 97t; Paul Schlemmer 100; shandrus 103;
Lichtmeister 106; Denphumi 114t; Radu Bercan 118; Gajus 123b; Rasstock 133; manaemedia 138; Bojana Ristic 139t; Furtseff 143b;
Ditty_about_summer 147b; Denphumi 150; Andrey_Popov 153; JJ pixs 155; Alexey Painter 156t; Joachim Wendler 172b; Tsyhun 174;
Moreno Soppelsa 176; CatchaSnap 177t; GrandeDuc 182b; ra2studio 184; Alexey Stiop 191; Dusit 194; Monkey Business Images 200b;
Nito 202; wrangler 204; Ivelin Radkov 206t; neelsky 208b; iQoncept 211b; Olga Besnard 217; Drazen 218; Marcel Mooij 220;
Enzodebernardo 223b; filmfoto 224; Peshkova 227; patpitchaya 230; Filipe Matos Frazao 237t; Blue SkyImage 239; FuzzBones 244;
Diego Cervo 246; alexskopje 247; alexskopje 250t.

SELF-PUBLISH YOUR NOVEL MADE EASY

RICHARD N. WILLIAMS

Foreword by REBECCA CANTRELL,
Amazon best-selling e-book author

**FLAME TREE
PUBLISHING**

CONTENTS

Publishing is changing – self-publishing is no longer a last resort, but a very real option for those who want to be independent of traditional publishers. This chapter introduces why self-publishing might just be the answer for both new and established writers.

Before you can publish, you must of course have something to put out there. As you begin to plan and write your book, understanding your genre and market is key, as well as thinking about your brand. This chapter covers all of this, as well as giving an overview of the different types of program you can use when writing and how to keep yourself motivated.

The digital age is changing many aspects of the book industry, including the way we read. Books can now be viewed on e-readers such as the Kindle, Nook or Kobo, as well as tablets and smartphones. This chapter examines how these different electronic devices present books, as well as the practicalities of formatting your work for various e-book platforms.

This chapter urges you not to believe the old saying 'don't judge a book by its cover'. It discusses why your cover should be eye-catching and professional and how to get it executed impeccably. It also goes on to cover what blurbs and metadata are and why they are essential for publicizing and selling your novel.

Wondering how to get your digital product out there? This chapter gives a step-by-step guide on how to sell your book online. You'll get an overview on pricing, as well as advice on growing your audience, and ensuring that you have a substantial amount of knowledge about uploading directly to vendors or getting a third party to do it for you. **Print-on-demand** services are also explored – while e-books are easy to distribute, there's nothing like having a printed copy of your novel in your hands.

MARKETING & SOCIAL MEDIA

Writing and distributing your book is only the first step to self-publishing. In order to take it to the next level, you will have to build an audience to make sales. In other words, you will have to market your novel. This chapter covers the importance of promoting and urges writers to promote their books before, during and after the novel is released. This promotion can be done through events as well as social media, which is a major tool for reaching readers.

THE BUSINESS OF SELF-PUBLISHING

Writing may be a hobby, but self-publishing is a business. The final chapter of this book takes you through the various legal issues involved in maintaining your rights and protecting your work. It also teaches you to think like a traditional publisher, handling all aspects of production and dealing with income and expenditure.

FOREWORD

THE WORLD BENEATH: A SELF-PUBLISHING SUCCESS

Why did I decide to self-publish my novel, *The World Beneath*? I've loved many things about being published by traditional publishers – seeing my books in stores, winning awards, and hitting the *New York Times* bestseller list – but one day I realized that my self-published friends were giddy in a way that I hadn't been since my first book.

They raved about creative control – setting your own schedule, picking your own cover, hiring an editor you trusted, and being able to solve publication problems on your own. They talked about financial control – determining how and when your book would be published, getting paid monthly and keeping the lion's share of the profits. They spoke of the joys of watching your backlist grow and work as hard for you as your most recently published book.

I was intrigued, but I was also daunted. What if I self-published my newly finished novel, *The World Beneath*, and no one wanted to read it? What if my New York friends sneered at me? What if I turned down an advance and never made that money back? What if I couldn't even make back the amount I paid for my cover designer and editor? Wasn't that like lighting cash on fire?

I agonized over it as only a neurotic writer can. Pros. Cons. Yes. No. Maybe. I made it into a much bigger and harder decision than it needed to be. Finally, I decided to give it a go because the constant *Sturm und Drang* was boring me. It was one book, one way, just to see.

Turns out it *was* just as fun as everyone said.

I loved having more control of the publication process. Readers did want to read the book. I made back enough to pay off my production costs. I made enough to cover that advance. And I'm still selling *The World Beneath*.

Self-publish Your Novel Made Easy will show you how to self-publish. I just want to reassure you that the decision to take that first step doesn't need to be big and scary. It's just one book, one way. Good luck!

Rebecca Cantrell, Amazon best-selling e-book author

INTRODUCTION

E-books have revolutionized publishing, which has now become accessible to far more people than before. This book is designed to help you self-publish your novel, find an audience and try to make money from your writing.

PUBLISHING YOUR NOVEL

Although all sorts of people have ambitions to write a novel, only a few of them ever put pen to paper. So what is it that puts so many off writing a book? Is it the prospect of having to submit their work to publishers and face rejections, or giving up creative control over their work? Whatever the reason, it no longer has to be that way: self-publishing has enabled all sorts of people to write and publish their novel while bypassing the traditional publishing model.

Inclusivity

Publishers can only publish a certain number of books each year. Traditionally, this meant that all sorts of great novels never made it into the hands of readers, and publishing remained accessible to only a select few. Self-publishing has changed all that, helping all aspiring authors to reach their audience.

Reputation of Self-publishing

Self-publishing used to be a byword for failure, with only those rejected by the mainstream publishing industry taking this route. However, that is no longer the case and nowadays, new writers find that self-publishing is a way for them to reach readers with their work; also, many established authors are now turning to self-publishing due to the many benefits that it offers.

WRITING YOUR NOVEL

This is a not a guide on how to write a novel. There are plenty of other books and online resources that can help you to structure your book, develop characters and create plots. However, we have included tips and strategies to help you find the time to write, and fit your writing and publishing around your normal daily activities. We have also included some handy hints on the different software to use for writing, formatting and converting your manuscript into e-book files.

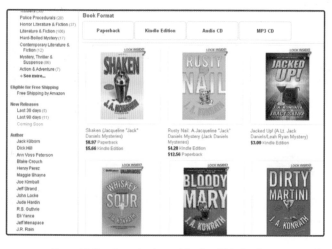

Above: J.A. Konrath, previously a traditionally published author, is now a well-known self-published author.

THIS BOOK

This book has been designed as a guide to help new writers to self-publish their first novel, as well as to assist more established authors who want to try a new way to reach readers. You may not want to read this book in one sitting, as it has been designed for you to use as a reference at each different stage of the self-publishing process. In it, you will find all sorts of useful information, ranging from helping you to get your book written to learning how to format, upload and distribute your work, as well as providing you with all the information you need to promote your book and find an audience.

SELF-PUBLISHING GUIDE

In this book, we will detail the advantages and disadvantages of self-publishing, and where self-publishing now sits in the overall publishing landscape. We will also guide you through the entire self-publishing process, providing you with all the information you will need to write your novel and bring it to market.

- **Writing your book**: We'll provide you with tips and techniques that can help you to structure your life so that you can find the time to write your novel.

- **Production**: You will learn about the different stages of e-book production that can help you turn your manuscript into a publishable book, including editing, proofing and cover design.

- **Format**: We'll show you how to convert your book into the various e-book formats, as well as how to produce printed editions of your novel.

- **Distribution**: You will find information on how to distribute your novel to the major e-book retailers, as well as how to promote your book and build an author platform.

Above: This book will guide you through distributing your book, including websites such as Amazon's KDP self-publishing platform.

STEP-BY-STEP

Both new writers and those already with a background in publishing will find this book useful, since we have tried to explain everything as clearly and simply as possible. Throughout the book, we have included step-by-step guides to steer you through some of the more complex processes of self-publishing, such as converting your files into e-book formats, creating e-book covers and using various promotional platforms such as social media networks.

Hot Tip

Throughout this book, we have inserted a number of Hot Tips. These are designed to help you find some simple yet effective methods to get the most out of self-publishing.

Terminology

Although self-publishing is full of its own jargon and terminology, where possible, we have provided instructions and information using the simplest terms and have explained some of the more complicated vocabulary.

Above: Unfamiliar terms such as ISBN, tags and metadata will be explained.

E-BOOK TECHNOLOGY

E-books and e-readers utilize different technologies. In this book, you will find explanations of the differences between the various e-book platforms and e-reading devices. We also describe how e-books differ from printed books and how to design your books to provide the best possible reading experience across the various formats.

'Print On Demand'

While e-books provide the simplest and most accessible way to self-publish, we also give you lots of useful information on how to convert your books into printed copies using print-on-demand services.

Left: Reach as many readers as possible by offering your work as both e–books and in print.

REACHING READERS

One of the hardest aspects of being a self-published author is finding readers. Without the promotional support of a large publisher, self-publishers have to promote their books by themselves. However, we will provide you with advice and information that can help you to reach as many readers as possible, as well as showing you how to build up your author platform so that you can turn writing into a viable career.

Author Income

While we cannot promise that you will become a bestselling author, it is certainly possible to make money by writing and self-publishing. We explain the business of publishing and give you all the information you will need in order to turn your writing into a profitable form of income.

HELP AND FURTHER READING

Since no book on self-publishing can possibly cover every conceivable aspect, we have included a list of helpful websites and other books for those wanting more information about certain aspects of writing and the self-publishing process.

SELF-PUBLISHIN

E-BOOKS
AUTHOR
COPYRIGHT
DISTRIBUTION

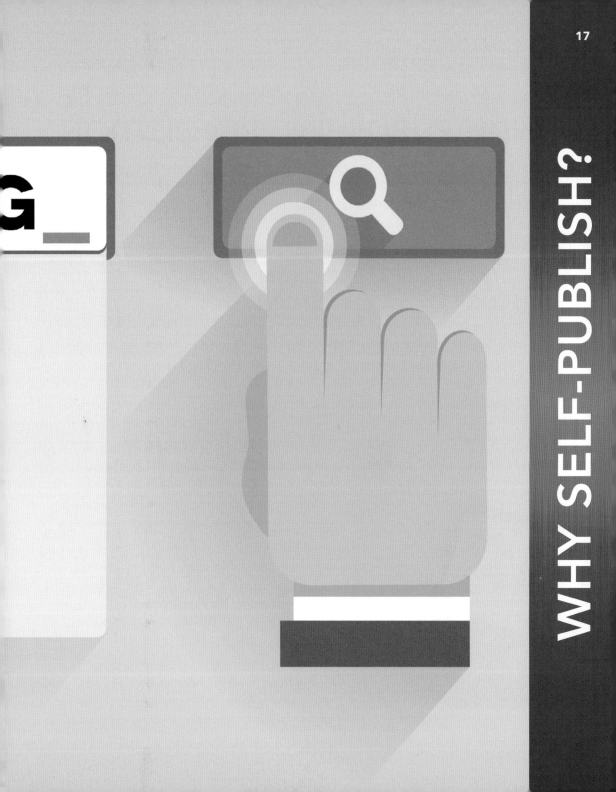

WHY SELF-PUBLISH?

INDIE PUBLISHING REVOLUTION

Publishing is changing: authors are now able to bypass traditional publishing houses and go it alone. Self-publishing has gone from the last resort for the rejected writer to a genuine alternative for authors who are attracted by the freedom and benefits offered by independent publishing.

HISTORY OF SELF-PUBLISHING

Self-publishing is nothing new. In 1901, tired of numerous rejections for her novel, aspiring children's author Beatrix Potter self-published *The Tales of Peter Rabbit*, which went on to be a huge success. After receiving 28 rejection letters, John Grisham, a lawyer from the United States, decided to create his own small press and printed 5,000 copies of his book, *A Time to Kill*. He eventually attracted the attention of a mainstream publisher and became a household name.

Self-publishing in the Digital Age

Self-publishing used to involve a lot of expense, with authors having to pay the costs of printing, distribution, storage and production costs, such as editing and cover design. However, digital technology has removed many of these expenses, making self-publishing a viable option for almost anybody.

Self-publishing Technology

Traditionally, publishing involved printing hundreds or thousands of books, but thanks to digital technology and the rise of the electronic book, there are now numerous ways for authors to bring their work to readers.

- **E-readers**: E-reading devices allow people to download and read electronic books (e-books) on a device that mimics the reading experience of a printed book.

- **Apps**: E-reading apps enable people to read e-books on tablet computers, mobile phones, laptops and desktop computers.

- **Print on demand (POD)**: Books that are printed individually, whenever somebody buys one, rather than in bulk.

- **Online**: You can publish a novel by simply posting it on a blog or website.

E-BOOK REVOLUTION

While there are various methods of self-publishing a book, by far the most revolutionary has been the rise of the e-book and the e-book reader.

E-readers

Although books have been available in formats such as PDF (Portable Document Format) for many years, reading them on a computer never proved popular. It was not until the development of dedicated e-book reading devices and tablet computers that publishing electronically became viable for both publishers and authors. These gadgets enable people to read electronic books when they are on the move or sitting in bed, just like a paper book. In addition, e-readers can store an entire library of books, making them extremely practical.

Hot Tip

E-books now make up a third of total book sales, with some people predicting that they will overtake the sale of printed books in the next few years.

Popular E-reading Devices

Different e-reading devices arrive on the market all the time, but several models have become extremely popular:

Above: Kindle on Amazon.com.

Above: The Nook homepage.

- **Amazon Kindle**: Amazon produces different types of Kindle, which are the most popular e-readers on the market.

- **Kobo**: This Canadian e-book provider produces one of the lowest-priced e-readers around.

- **Nook**: Sold by American bookstore Barnes & Noble.

- **Sony Reader**: Versatile e-readers that can read various e-book formats.

- **Tablet computers**: Many tablet computers, such as Apple's iPad, make excellent e-reading devices.

E-book Distribution

The big advantage of e-books for authors and publishers is that they do not involve any of the high production costs associated with printed books. Rather than printing hundreds or thousands of books, storing them in a warehouse and distributing them to bookshops across the nation, an author or publisher can create an e-book file and upload it directly to online vendors, enabling readers to purchase and download the book directly to their e-reading devices.

E-book Vendors

Some of the most popular online e-book vendors include the following:

- **Amazon**: The world's biggest online book retailer, it sells more e-books than all the other vendors combined.

- **iBookstore**: Apple's iBookstore enables iTunes users to download e-books for their Apple devices.

- **Sony**: Sony's bookstore sells e-books aimed for use with the Sony Reader or on computers and phones using a Sony Reader app.

- **Kobo**: Has its own online bookstore, but also supplies e-books to several retailers, including WH Smith in the UK.

Above: The Amazon Kindle store.

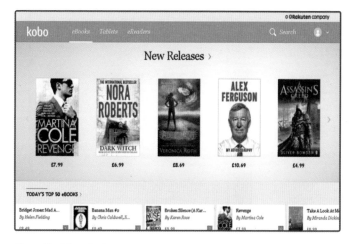

Above: The Kobo e-book store.

○ **Barnes & Noble:** As the United States' largest high street bookstore, Barnes & Noble also has a popular e-book store.

THE SELF-PUBLISHING MODEL

Self-publishing offers almost anybody the opportunity to publish a book. Using the traditional publishing model, if you had written a novel, you had to send your manuscript to a literary agent who, if they felt the book had potential, would attempt to sell it to a publisher. If a publishing house liked it, they would normally pay you an advance before editing, printing and distributing your book.

> ## Hot Tip
> Aggregator services such as Smashwords will distribute your book to most of the major e-book retailers, so you do not have to approach them individually.

Above: Smashwords is an example of an e-book aggregator, which will distribute your book to major e-book retailers.

Author to Reader

This route to finding a publisher always requires a lot of luck, time and perseverance. Publishing houses cannot publish every book submitted to them, so they have the unenviable task of selecting only those books that they think have the most potential. Inevitably, they do not always get it right and many of today's bestselling authors will have accumulated dozens of rejection slips from publishers and agents along the way. In addition, books selected by publishing houses are not always successful. Self-publishing has enabled authors to

Hot Tip

Many literary agents and publishers often look for successful self-published titles on websites such as Amazon to see if they are worth signing up for a publishing deal.

bypass publishers and agents, allowing them to reach readers without having to go through a selection process first.

INDIE PUBLISHING

While it is possible for you to do everything, few self-published authors have found success without ensuring that their book is properly edited and formatted. For this reason, many authors refer to the process as independent publishing, as they have not gone through the traditional publishing route but have not done it alone, and may have hired editors, formatters, cover designers and other help to produce their books.

Mainstream Indie Publishing

Indie publishing has attracted much criticism, with some arguing that many self-published titles lack the quality of traditionally published books. However, attitudes to self-publishing are slowly changing. Many traditionally published authors are now choosing to publish their work independently because of the many advantages it offers over the traditional route (more on this later). In addition, indie publishing has produced many bestselling authors, and self-published books are regularly entering mainstream bestseller lists.

Self-publishing Successes

Indie publishing has produced numerous success stories. Some of these people have gone on to sign multimillion-dollar book deals with traditional publishers, while others have chosen to continue to publish independently.

- **John Locke:** The first self-published author to sell over one million e-books on Amazon. John Locke went on to sell the paperback distribution rights to New York publishers Simon and Schuster and has become a *New York Times* bestseller.

○ **Amanda Hocking**: Having written 17 novels in her spare time but unable to secure a publisher, she self-published her books and sold more than a million copies before signing a traditional publishing deal with St Martin's Press.

○ **Hugh Howey**: The success of his self-published short story, *Wool*, on Amazon encouraged him to expand his story into a series. He eventually sold over a million copies, signed the print rights to Simon and Schuster and also attracted interest from film director Ridley Scott to turn the series into a film.

○ **E.L. James**: Originally a fan fiction writer who published her work on her own website, E.L. James went on to write *Fifty Shades of Grey*, which became the most commercially successful novel in history.

SELF-PUBLISHING REALITIES

The rise of self-publishing has been phenomenal, and indie-published books now make up 12 per cent of all e-book sales. However, despite the headline successes, self-publishing is not an easy path to fame and riches and the actual reality is rather more sobering.

- **Competition**: An estimated one million books are published each year; three-quarters of these are self-published, reprints of public-domain works and other print-on-demand books.

- **Earnings**: Only 10 per cent of self-published authors earn more than $7,500 (£4,700) a year; over half earn less than $500 (£300).

- **Sales**: Nearly half of all self-published books sell fewer than 250 copies.

Defining Success

Of course, the situation is not that much better for traditionally published authors. Few people are able to make a living writing fiction, while even fewer go on to become bestsellers. However, success can mean different things to different people: some self-published authors are finding that they are selling enough books to pay some of their bills each month, while others are just happy that they are now able to reach readers.

Above: Self-publishing can be difficult, but there are different methods to measure success.

IDENTIFYING YOUR GOALS

Some authors wish to carve out a career by writing, while others are happy generating a modest part-time income and some just want to reach as many readers as possible. Identifying your goals is important before you commit to any form of publishing.

WHAT DO YOU WANT TO ACHIEVE?

Self-publishing is a viable alternative to the traditional publishing model, but you need to know why you want to self-publish in the first place. You need to reflect on what you want out of self-publishing so that you can work out how best you can achieve it.

For success, make sure your goals are the following:

- **Clear**: Make sure you know what you want to achieve, whether it be to reach a set number of readers or to make a certain amount of money.

- **Achievable**: Most writers would love to be a bestseller or make millions from their books, but this is more a dream than an ambition; keep your goals realistic.

- **Measurable**: Plan a timeline and select a date by which you want to make a certain amount of money or sell a certain number of books. This way, you can identify how far from or close you are to achieving your goals.

Hot Tip

Most self-publishers do not achieve their goals with their first book. Think long-term and plan to increase sales/readers with each subsequent book.

Prioritizing Your Writing

No matter what you want to achieve, you need to assess how writing and publishing fit in with your day-to-day life. You may have a full-time job, a family or other commitments which could affect how achievable your goals are.

- **Time**: Writing and self-publishing require a lot of time. Most people have personal commitments, so you need to ensure that you have enough time to dedicate to your work.

Above: Set timelines for reaching your goals.

○ **Money:** You may need to hire help for things such as formatting, editing and cover design. Make sure you can afford the expense, as it may be many months, or even years, before you see a return on your investment.

○ **Work:** Self-publishing takes a lot of hard work and commitment, and requires you to learn new skills – be prepared for that.

UNDERSTANDING WHAT'S IN STORE

Whatever your goal, self-publishing is not for everyone and, depending on what you want to achieve, you may be better off looking to the traditional model of publishing. There are many different aspects to producing a book and, without the support of a publisher, you have to do much of it yourself. Some authors would rather just write than have to think about the following matters:

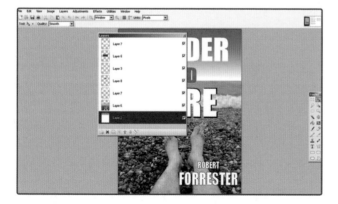

Above: An eye-catching cover is key to selling your book.

○ **Editing:** All books need to be presented in as good a form as possible, which means being free from errors.

○ **Formatting:** Even a digital book has to be formatted correctly.

○ **Cover design:** All books need an engaging and eye-catching cover.

- **Marketing**: You cannot expect readers to stumble across your book, which means that you need to market and promote your work.

- **Distribution**: Self-published authors have to distribute their own work, as well as keeping track of sales and costs.

Hot Tip

By learning to do as many of the aspects relating to self-publishing yourself, you can reduce costs. You can also 'trade' services, such as proofreading and editing, with other self-published authors.

Expectations

Few self-published authors are able to sell hundreds or thousands of copies of their books straightaway. While overnight successes happen, they are the exception rather than the rule. Anybody who wants to reach readers, generate an income or carve out a career by self-publishing needs to think about the long-term and prepare for hiccups along the way. At first, you may receive negative reviews and poor sales, or struggle to get to grips with many of the aspects of self-publishing. Be patient and do not expect too much too soon.

Making the Right Decision

Self-publishing involves a lot of work, so you need to think carefully before committing yourself. Ask yourself whether it is the right path for you and your book, and make sure that your decision is based on the right reasons. Self-publishing is neither an easy way to publishing success nor a last resort just because you cannot get your book published by traditional publishers.

ADVANTAGES OF SELF-PUBLISHING

Self-publishing used to be a last resort for authors. However, digital publishing and online e-book retailers have meant that not only is self-publishing now a viable alternative for many authors, but it also offers numerous advantages over the traditional publishing route.

THE FREEDOM OF SELF-PUBLISHING

Not having a publisher means that authors have the freedom to make all the decisions about their book and their writing. This control enables an author to write and publish what they want and not what a publisher wants them to produce.

Hot Tip

You can self-publish under various pen names and use a different one for each genre. This will enable you to build up a number of different audiences and will mean that your readers won't become confused or disappointed.

Genre

Many traditionally published authors find that they are pigeonholed into a particular genre. Publishers are reluctant to allow these authors to write in other genres because they are a known quantity in a particular field, and branching out poses too much of a risk. Self-publishers have none of these restrictions and are free to write in multiple genres if they wish.

Add or Change contributors				×
First (or Given) name:	Last name (or Surname):	Title:		
John	Smith	Author	▾	Remove
Add another				
			Save	Cancel

Left: You are not restricted to publishing under your real name; you can choose your own pen name.

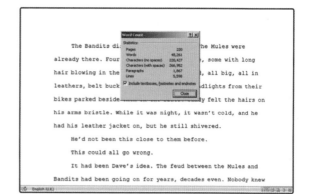

Hot Tip

Before you attempt a full-length novel, why not write and self-publish a few short stories? This is a great way to improve your writing while helping you to get to grips with the self-publishing process.

Length

Publishers have always expected books to be a certain length, partly because of cover price versus the cost of paper and ink. Few people will want to pay full price for a book that is only half the length of a similar work. In addition, certain conventions regarding length have developed around different genres, thus forcing authors to write to a minimum and maximum word count. Shorter works, such as novellas and short stories, are rarely published by traditional houses, but with self-publishing, especially to e-book, authors can write to any length they wish.

Deadlines

Traditional publishers work to a rigid publishing schedule. If an author is contracted to write a certain number of books or submit revisions on a novel, there will more than likely be a deadline to hand in this work. Self-publishers are able to write and publish according to a time frame that suits them.

Above: Writing short stories can be a good start, before attempting longer novels.

THE SPEED OF SELF-PUBLISHING

Getting a book published can take time. Not only does a novel take many months – even years – to write, but it can also take just as long to find an agent and publisher willing to take the project on. Once you have signed a publishing contract, it may still be a long time before your work sees the light of day. It could take up to two years from the time you sign your contract before the book is finally printed and released. With self-publishing, though, you can get a book to market a lot more quickly, because you do not have to worry about the following issues:

- **Querying**: You don't need to spend time looking for a publisher or agent.

- **Editorial**: You can arrange your own editorial services and therefore won't have to wait for your publisher to edit and format your book.

- **Release date**: You can choose your release date, opting for a time that suits you.

- **Distribution**: With digital publishing, it takes just a few hours to upload your book and have it available for sale, rather than waiting for weeks for books to be printed and shipped.

Above: KDP publishing screen, showing that it takes less than 12 hours before a book goes live.

CREATIVE CONTROL

One of the biggest advantages many authors find with indie publishing is the creative control they have over the process. Self-published authors have the final say on any decisions.

Editorial Control

If you have sold a novel to a publishing house, an editor may wish for you to make certain changes. Often, these can help to improve the book, but many decisions can be subjective and,

although many of them are open to discussion, the editor normally has the final say. Self-published authors hire their own editors, so can opt to make changes depending on whether or not they agree with them.

Covers and Marketing

Self-published authors have complete control over how a book is marketed, including decisions on cover design and product information. In traditional publishing, this is usually not the case, which can mean that an author might end up with a cover that they hate.

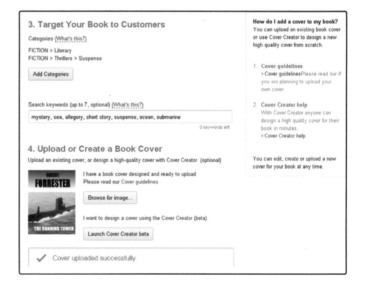

Above: The Kindle Direct Publishing dashboard, where you can upload covers and include different categories and other marketing information.

ROYALTIES

One of the main reasons why many established authors have opted to self-publish their work is the greater royalty rate they get per book. Due to the costs associated with a publishing house, authors often receive less than 10 per cent royalties on the price of a book. By self-publishing, though, authors can earn much higher royalties, with vendors such as Amazon paying up to 70 per cent on the cover price of an e-book.

Payment made to:	RICHARD WILLIAMS(DWMN4)
Our Supplier No.:	13426853
Supplier site name:	DWMN4_GBP
Payment number:	8450398
Payment date:	29-OCT-2013
Payment currency:	GBP
Payment amount:	447.29

Invoice Number	Invoice Date	Invoice Description	Discount Taken	Amount Paid	Amount Remaining
6H0-DIGITAL-NA5NBPK91D3N1ZK9XFZ0	29-SEP-2013	Aug 2013 Kindle Direct Publishing payment		18.80	0.00
6H1-DIGITAL-5MHPPHHSECFBR8A11YX1	29-SEP-2013	Aug 2013 Kindle Direct Publishing payment		9.90	0.00
6H2-DIGITAL-FNNAPP4QFGQ9K827TC00	29-SEP-2013	Aug 2013 Kindle Direct Publishing payment		7.55	0.00
6H3-DIGITAL-7YFSP9OX28TZYKXZAHZ0	29-SEP-2013	Aug 2013 Kindle Direct Publishing payment		15.42	0.00
6H4-DIGITAL-XP8F6576ZZP05B3RCTM1	29-SEP-2013	Aug 2013 Kindle Direct Publishing payment		20.77	0.00
6HA-DIGITAL-63ZJF8FHD8HZ3FZ0OJO0	29-SEP-2013	Aug 2013 Kindle Direct Publishing payment		8.80	0.00
6HB-DIGITAL-E04AHW8P15GQ4O2OX5M1	29-SEP-2013	Aug 2013 Kindle Direct Publishing payment		11.71	0.00
6HC-DIGITAL-15WVCTV6QH35ZYEMK7Y1	29-SEP-2013	Aug 2013 Kindle Direct Publishing payment		12.14	0.00
6HD-DIGITAL-1QWHNGTYC8BJKY2D96D1	29-SEP-2013	Aug 2013 Kindle Direct Publishing payment		6.53	0.00
6HE-DIGITAL-RM9WNVJPEBJJ02A4SFP0	29-SEP-2013	Aug 2013 Kindle Direct Publishing payment		8.07	0.00
6HF-DIGITAL-XNM7R82XAEKWF8Z1XWR1	29-SEP-2013	Aug 2013 Kindle Direct Publishing payment		9.55	0.00

Above: Amazon sends authors a monthly royalty remittance slip.

Payment Frequency

Another big bonus for self-published authors is the frequency with which vendors make their payments. In some cases, such as with Amazon, authors are paid monthly, whereas in traditional publishing, it is common practice to pay royalties every six months.

Hot Tip

Selling through websites such as Amazon, Kobo and Smashwords enables you to track your sales daily, so that you can see just how many copies you have sold and work out how much money you have made each week.

NO SUBMISSIONS

There are no entrance barriers with self-publishing: you do not need an agent and you do not need to chase a publishing house. Although many manuscripts sent to publishers and agents may not be of a high enough quality to publish, many still are. This has led to many talented authors accumulating dozens and even hundreds of rejections before finding a home for their work. All this takes time, but with self-publishing, you can bring a book to market without having to satisfy somebody else's opinion as to whether or not they think it will sell.

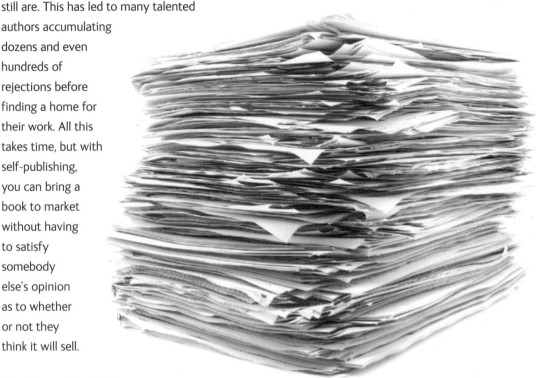

The New Slush Pile

Publishers and agents receive hundreds of manuscript submissions each week, which are referred to as the 'slush pile', and, due to the sheer volume, it can be notoriously difficult to get your manuscript noticed. However, an increasing number of publishers and agents are signing up self-published authors with a proven track record, which has made this a viable way to avoid the slush pile and find a traditional publisher, if that is your goal.

Hot Tip

Many agents will now work with successful self-published authors and help them to sell overseas rights, as well as dealing with any options for film rights.

RIGHTS

When you sell a novel to a publishing house, you are actually selling the rights to the work. This means that a publisher will have exclusive rights to publish the work in a certain territory, which can often last for many years, no matter how many or how few books you are selling. With some publishing contracts, you may even lose the rights to your work for the life of its copyright. By self-publishing, you retain all rights to your book, thus enabling you to do whatever you wish with it.

Contracts

Although a self-published author has to abide by any contracts laid down by vendors, these are not nearly as restrictive as contracts from publishing houses. Some publishing contracts include non-compete clauses, which prevent authors from writing other books in the same genre, or first option clauses, which automatically entitle the publisher to the rights to your next book.

FLEXIBILITY

Indie publishing offers authors unrivalled flexibility. They can choose where to sell their books and for what price, and they can make all sorts of changes without having to go through a publisher.

Revisions

One of the great advantages of digital publishing is the ability to make amendments and revisions. With a traditionally printed book, if an author spots an error or typographical mistake, he or she has to wait until the next printing to get it changed. With an e-book or POD title, however, mistakes can be rectified as soon as they are spotted, with new revised editions uploaded and available for sale in a matter of hours.

Above: Digital publishing allows for updates and revisions to be uploaded easily.

Experimentation

Self-publishers are also free to experiment and try different things. If a book is not selling very well, it is possible to lower the price, do a promotion or give away copies for free, as well as trying out new covers, product descriptions, categories and keywords.

INFORMED

Authors can be quite insecure and like to know how popular their books are. With traditional publishing, it can be extremely difficult to get accurate information, as sales figures are often many months out of date. Self-published authors have far easier access to this information. Many vendors provide daily sales figures and monthly reports, and you can even see in what country people are buying your book.

> ## Hot Tip
> Many online vendors have ranking systems for both books and authors. This enables the latter to check how popular their books are compared to others in the same genre.

Analytics

Some vendors (for example, Smashwords) provide statistical information, such as the number of page views your book's product page has received, how many readers have downloaded a sample and how many have made an actual purchase. You can even receive email updates whenever somebody has bought a book or left a review.

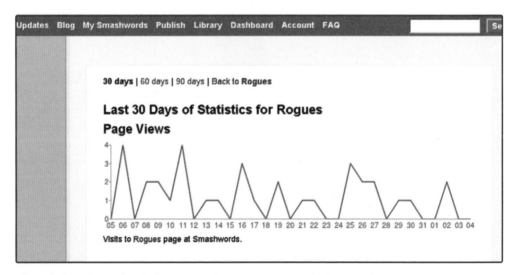

Above: Vendors such as Smashwords allow you to view how many times your page has been viewed.

PERSONAL SATISFACTION

All authors – no matter how they are published – should be proud of their work, of course, but having done it all by yourself can bring tremendous satisfaction. Having written and created your own book means you'll experience an even greater sense of accomplishment.

New Skills

Indie publishing will encourage you to learn many new skills. These include practical things, such as creating covers or designing page layouts, as well as learning a little about business, hiring third-party help, negotiating fees and taking responsibility for an entire project.

Community

Writing can be a lonely vocation, but self-published authors find that they are part of a larger group. You will discover that the indie-publishing community is very friendly and all too willing to help out and offer advice. All sorts of forums, websites and social media groups are available, where you can share your experiences and learn from other self-published writers.

Above: Self-publishing forums are an excellent place to look for advice.

DISADVANTAGES OF SELF-PUBLISHING

Self-publishing requires a lot of work, time and commitment. It is also fraught with challenges and pitfalls. For some authors, the disadvantages of self-publishing can outweigh its advantages.

ON YOUR OWN

Self-publishing can be scary. There are many steps involved in turning your manuscript into a professional-looking book, and for a lot of people, the prospect of going it alone can be daunting. For this reason, you need a certain amount of confidence and self-belief to become an indie publisher.

Support

If you publish through a traditional publisher, you will find you have a lot of support and a whole network of help around you, such as editors, agents and marketing professionals. Self-published authors are on their own, which can make it a lonely experience, especially for first-time novelists.

Hot Tip

Join a writing group or link up with other self-published authors on the internet in order to find people who understand your problems and can offer guidance.

Left: Join online writing groups to find a support network of other self–published authors.

Editorial Services

One of the biggest hurdles and disadvantages that self-publishers face is the lack of any editorial support. A traditional publishing house will provide everything you need to bring a book to market, including editing, copy-editing, cover creation, formatting and marketing. A self-published author has to either arrange for third-party help or do these things themselves.

No Vested Interest

Finding good help can be difficult. One of the big differences between hiring editorial services and those being provided by a publishing house is that a freelancer has no stake in your book. In other words, they have nothing to gain or lose, whether the book is successful or not. At a publishing house, it is in everybody's interest to ensure that a book is as good as it can be.

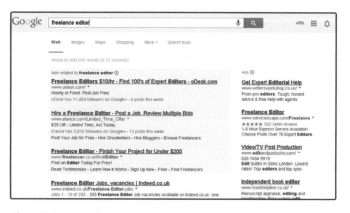

Above: Finding a good freelance editor is important.

Editors at publishing houses have their reputations to think of, and the publisher will have a financial commitment to the project. This means that they will not want to bring a book to market if it is not going to succeed.

ADVANCES AND COSTS

When you sign up with a traditional publisher, you are normally awarded an advance. This is a sum of money paid in lieu of royalties from potential book sales and can range from a few thousand pounds, or dollars, to six-figure sums. They mean that an author has a source of revenue before the book is even released. Advances can provide the necessary funds to write the next book, and in some cases can allow an author to give up their job and work full time on their writing. Even if sales are not as expected, authors are not usually asked to repay advances.

kindle direct publishing   Bookshelf | **Reports** | Community | KDP Select

1. Month-to-Date Unit Sales
View your unit sales transactions for the current and prior month.

2. Prior Six Weeks' Royalties
View your royalties for the past six weeks.

3. Prior Months' Royalties
View your royalties for the past 12 months. These reports are generated by the 15th day of the month.

4. Promotions
View the performance of your Kindle Countdown Deals promotions (updated periodically as your promotion runs).

View report for: Amazon.fr   Search [   ] GO View all

Week	Title	Author	ASIN	Units Sold	Units Refunded	Net Units Sold	Royalty Type	Transaction Type	

There are no sales to report during this pe

Above: It can take quite a while for self–published authors to make money from their books.

Earnings

Self-published authors do not have an advance and will start with no income. It is only when you begin selling books that you will see any money. Sales may be slow initially, or non-existent, so it could take months or even years before you see any earnings, and the hard truth is that some self-published authors never earn enough in royalties to match the sort of money that publishers offer in advances.

Expenses

Securing a traditional publisher means that you will not have to pay anything upfront, as publishers pay for all the costs of producing the book. However, self-publishing means that you may have to pay for various services needed to bring your book to market, which can include the following:

Hot Tip

Do not be afraid to negotiate costs from third parties. Stick to your budget, and do not overspend, as it may be a while before you see a return on your investment.

- **Editorial:** Editing costs can vary, depending on whether you opt for a simple proofread or extensive copy-editing, but it normally runs into several hundreds of pounds or dollars.

- **Cover design:** A professional-looking cover is essential, so unless you have an artistic streak, prepare to pay a few hundred pounds or dollars for a good book cover.

Formatting: If you cannot learn to format your book, you will need to hire a professional formatter, which will cost roughly another £100 (around $60).

Promotional services: If you want to run advertisements or use promotional services, such as Bookbub, you will have to budget for this too. Advertising prices can range from £30 ($50) to several hundred.

LEGITIMACY

Self-publishing has always had a stigma attached to it. Despite the headline successes and the number of traditionally published authors who are now opting to self-publish, many people do not regard indie-published books as having the same legitimacy as books published by traditional publishers. Few self-published authors receive the same plaudits, and most literary agents, publishers and literary magazines do not regard self-published authors as being properly 'published'.

Above: The Man Booker Prize is not open to self–published authors.

Above: Reviews of self–published works rarely appear in mainstream publications like *The New York Times*.

Reviews

Mainstream publications, such as newspapers and journals, rarely review self-published work. This means that you are unlikely to see your book in *The New York Times* or *Guardian*. TV and radio stations are also unlikely to want to interview you as a self-published author.

Awards and Associations

If you are dreaming of winning the Man Booker Prize, being shortlisted for a Hugo Award or joining a writing association such as the Science Fiction & Fantasy Writers of America (SFWA), there is very little chance of this happening to you as a self-published author. Authors who self-publish are not eligible for most awards and few organizations accept them as members.

MARKETING

Publishing houses have lots of influence and big budgets, which they can spend on promotion and marketing. While not every traditionally published author will find their work advertised on billboards or in national newspapers, publishers will do a lot of work to promote a book. On the other hand, going it alone means that all the promotion and marketing work is down to you.

> ## Hot Tip
> Be careful how you approach promotion! Many people will soon tire of you if all you talk about on social media is your book. You also run the risk of coming across as desperate if you over-promote.

Promotion

Many self-published authors find that they spend more time promoting and marketing their books than they do writing. Blogging, social media interaction and sending books off to review websites can be time-consuming. There is no magic formula to book promotion, either: some books sell well with very little marketing, while some authors spend hours and hours promoting their books only to see no upturn in sales.

Above: Social media is an invaluable tool; but be careful not to over-promote.

REACH

For many published authors, there is nothing more satisfying than seeing their work on the shelves of the local bookshop or library. Self-published authors rarely get the same satisfaction. It is doubtful whether you are going to see your novel in the local supermarket, chain store, airport bookshop or local library. In fact, most self-published authors sell their work solely on the internet, and even those with print titles still find that the majority of their sales are in e-book format.

Bookstore Sales

Although e-books are now hugely popular and more and more people choose to buy books on the internet, the high street sector still makes up a large chunk of the market. For most

Hot Tip

If you have created a POD print book, why not approach your local bookshop and see if they would be willing to stock a few copies? They can only say no.

self-published authors, bookstore chains, supermarkets and other print outlets are out of reach. This means that you have a smaller potential share of the market than traditional publishers do.

Discoverability

While not exclusively a problem faced by self-publishers, without the ability to market books in bookstores and other venues, getting your work discovered by readers is incredibly difficult. With thousands of books self-published each week, as well as all those produced by publishing companies, it is very easy for your work to get lost amongst the sea of other titles.

Lone Voice

Without the support of a publisher, who can perhaps get a book reviewed or can arrange interviews and other promotional events on an author's behalf, self-publishers face the challenge of bringing a book to an already congested marketplace, where tens of thousands of other lone voices are also attempting to be heard.

Hard Work

All this means that self-published authors have to work a lot harder to get their book noticed than traditionally published authors do. If you are unwilling to spend

Above: Self-published authors have to work hard to promote their books in an already congested marketplace.

time promoting or just want to write books and not worry about all the other aspects of publishing, then self-publishing is probably not for you.

RESPONSIBILITY

Although self-publishing means that you will experience the satisfaction of knowing that you have achieved it all on your own, the reverse is also true. While traditionally published authors can always complain that their publisher let them down, the cover wasn't right or they did not get the marketing support they needed, by going it alone, you may only have yourself to blame if your books fail to sell or you receive negative reviews.

Stress

This responsibility can make self-publishing extremely stressful. Being a self-publisher means that you are essentially running your own publishing company, albeit one with only one author. This means that you have to take

Above: Seeing zero sales can be disappointing, but perseverance is key.

responsibility for every stage of the process: from hiring the right people to choosing the price, the cover and the venues to sell your book. Many self-publishers have high expectations for their work, only to become deeply disappointed when things do not turn out as they had planned.

Learning Curve

Without the support of a publisher, you may find that you spend far more time doing other things than you spend writing. Many of these tasks take up valuable time.

- **Book production**: Not only do you have to write a book; you also need to get it edited, proofed and formatted, as well as choosing a cover and writing a product description.

- **Distribution**: You have to distribute your own book, which means learning how to upload your work to different vendors.

- **Promotion**: With thousands of other books being self-published every week, you have to learn how to promote your work effectively.

- **Business**: You have to treat self-publishing as a business, which means learning to do many of the tasks that business owners carry out, such as keeping a record of your expenses and sales, as well as paying any relevant taxes.

Hot Tip

Do not be in too much of a hurry to self-publish your book. Make sure that you are 100 per cent happy with it before you bring it to market.

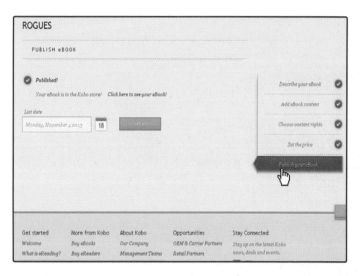

Above: Make sure you are completely ready before publishing.

ravine down a few feet away and was
The weather was icy and cold, he
only hugged his cigarettes and flask

"As I sat there waiting, I f
watch laying on top the ground
up but it was kind of stuck." He
the rest of his story after a c

"After scratching at the sandy
watch was stuck to the spot be

Lucas was shocked to he
lot of time out in the area
the ct Drilling Co. They ha
exploration. They worked a
Divide Basin, punching hol
company and Lucas enjoyed
he had to take over the
father suffered a strok

Lucas' son, Wade,
old Chevy pick-up. Luc
from Wade then jumped
conversation by Wade
huh from his dad. Fi
only minutes before
"I am stunned." Wa
that old dry cow

WRITING YOUR BOOK

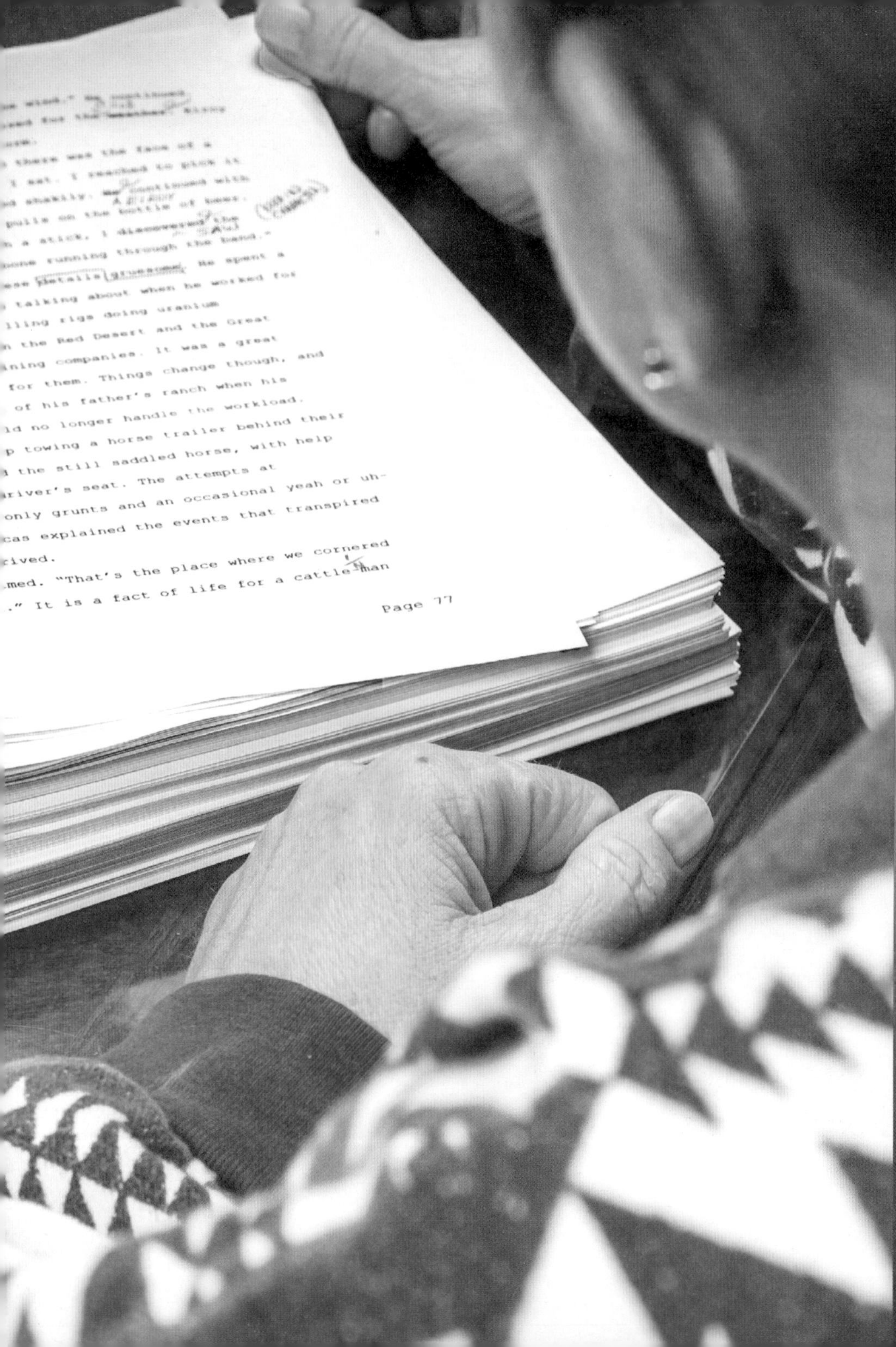

THE RIGHT GENRE

Before you start writing a novel, it is important to understand who your audience will be. Novels fall into different categories, known as genres, and before you can bring any book to market, you need to understand where it belongs.

UNDERSTANDING GENRE

Genre is simply a term that describes different categories of fiction. You can define nearly all novels into one or more specific genres, and here are some of the most popular fiction ones.

- **Mysteries:** Often crime-related. These sorts of stories usually follow characters around, such as sleuths or detectives, as they try to solve a mystery.

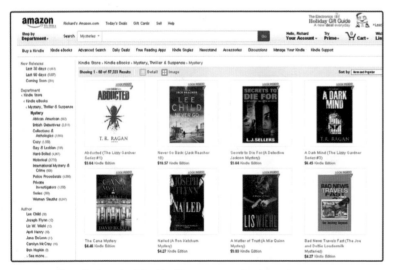

Above: Books can be defined by different genres, such as 'mystery'.

- **Thriller:** Fast-paced stories that feature suspense, tension and excitement. Thrillers often contain a lot of action too.

- **Horror:** Stories designed to frighten or shock readers. Horror stories can involve psychological fear or be gory in content.

○ **Science fiction**: Often future-related or space-based. These stories explore science and technology, or examine potential utopian or dystopian societies.

○ **Fantasy**: Stories that are often based in imaginary worlds or in contemporary settings where magic or supernatural activities take place.

○ **Romance**: Novels where the story centres on the romantic relationship between two (or more) characters.

○ **Historical**: Fiction based in historical settings, such as the Roman Empire or medieval Britain.

Purpose of Genre

Genres are a way to categorize books to make it easier for readers to find stories that they enjoy reading. Many readers have genre preferences so may only wish to read novels of a certain type. Genres also enable bookstores and online retailers to assemble books that have similar styles and conventions together.

GENRE CONVENTIONS

Genre plays more of a role than just compartmentalizing books. Readers expect books of a certain genre to share similarities, so before writing a novel, it is important to understand what these conventions are in order to ensure that you are writing something that your audience wants.

Above: Mills & Boon produce lots of romance books, many of which are similar in style.

Style and Themes

Genre can influence how a book is written. For instance, romance authors tend to use lots of adjectives and descriptive prose in their books and explore themes of love, jealousy and relationships, whereas thriller writers usually write tight, concise prose and explore basic themes of good versus evil and triumph over adversity.

Hot Tip

When deciding on which genre to write in, think about the books that you like reading and work out which genre they fall under.

Form

Genre also goes a long way to influence the form of a novel. Mysteries and romantic fiction tend to be shorter than thrillers and science fiction novels, while historical fiction and fantasy books are often much longer. Readers also expect certain genres, such as thrillers, to be fast-paced, whereas genres such as romance tend to have a more sedate story arc.

Story Conventions

Most genre writers also follow conventions when it comes to the actual stories. In mysteries, the crime needs to be solved; protagonists in thrillers have to save the day; and the girl should always get the guy in a romance book. Of course, some authors can get away with breaking these conventions, but most new writers should stick to them.

Marketing

Genre also affects the marketing of a book. The demographics for different genres can differ dramatically. For instance, the majority of readers of romance books are female, which means that everything from the product description to the cover design has to appeal to women readers.

Above: Romance books often have a handsome man on the cover to appeal to female readers.

Literary Fiction

Books often excluded from genre and its conventions are known as literary fiction. Some people argue that literary fiction is in itself just another genre, but others contest that this type of fiction is defined by its literary merit and includes deeper themes, subtexts and multilayered stories than genre stories.

Hot Tip

Before you begin writing, read plenty of books in your intended genre and make sure you understand the conventions of style, content and form.

GENRE TITLES

The title of a book is also greatly affected by genre. For instance, thrillers need a short, exciting title, while horror novels need an unnerving title. Your book's title is a very powerful tool for encouraging readers to buy it. Titles also have a role to play in discoverability, especially as most online bookstores utilize search engines.

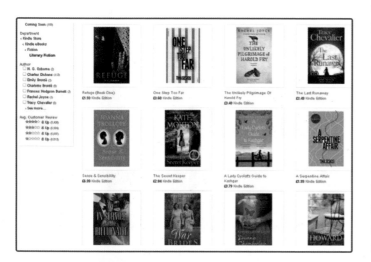

Above: Literary fiction titles on Amazon, which are hard to categorize.

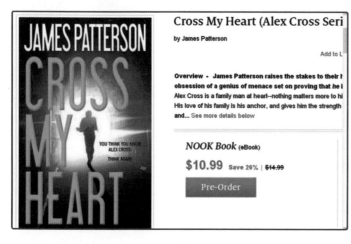

Above: Subtitles are common in thriller genres.

Choosing a Title

Coming up with your book's title is not easy. Some authors use tried-and-tested titles, known as stock titles. These are usually short two- or three-word titles that briefly describe what a book is about, such as *The Warrior*, *Summer of Love* or *Murder in ...* (add a location). However, in order to increase your appeal to readers, it is best to come up with something unique.

Choosing a Subtitle

It is now common in some genres for books to have a subtitle, which can engage the reader with a brief catch-line describing what the work is about. Subtitles often invoke suspense and intrigue. In

Hot Tip

Write down all the words that describe what your book is about, including character names and places, and then put some of these words together to form a list of two- or three-word titles.

addition, they are great for inserting keywords and other search terms that will help readers to find your book when they are using search engines.

SUBGENRES

When the only place to buy books was the local bookshop, genres used to be quite broad-based. All mysteries were placed in the mystery section and all science fiction was on the sci-fi shelves. However, online bookselling has allowed authors and readers to be more specific when it comes to genre, and a whole raft of subgenres has developed.

Subcategories

If you visit any online retailer and click on the various genre categories, you will see a list of numerous subcategories. These allow readers to find the books they like more easily, while also enabling authors to aim their work at more specific audiences.

Cross-genre

Sometimes, it can be very difficult to categorize a book, even with the huge

Science Fiction
- Adventure (17,954)
- Alien Invasion (1,020)
- Alternative History (3,637)
- Anthologies & Short Stories (8,360)
- Classics (387)
- Colonization (717)
- Cyberpunk (747)
- Dystopian (3,134)
- First Contact (531)
- Galactic Empire (560)
- Genetic Engineering (1,376)
- Hard Science Fiction (3,960)
- Metaphysical & Visionary (1,409)
- Military (4,010)

Ep.#9 - "Resistance" (The Frontiers Saga)
$3.07 Kindle Edition

Above: The sci-fi genre on Amazon has several further subcategories to choose from.

number of subgenres now available. Indeed, some authors like to experiment and use conventions of two or more genres, thus creating what is known as a cross-genre novel. Often, if these books become successful, they end up spawning a new subgenre.

WRITING TO GENRE

Some people hate the idea of genre, and find the idea of writing to specific conventions and form restrictive. Genre writing means that you have to select your characters and themes carefully, but it also has its advantages.

Hot Tip

If you cannot make up your mind as to which genre to write in, make a pros and cons list and write the positives and negatives of each genre.

- **Defined market:** People are more likely to read a book that is a known quantity than something that is experimental.

Above: Online retailers have different bestseller lists for each subgenre.

- **Process:** Writing within rules and conventions can often be easier when it comes to planning your work. Knowing the way a book has to end, such as the hero saving the day, makes it much easier to finish a novel than trying to think of a surprise ending.

- **Platform:** It is far easier to build an audience platform if you are writing in a specific genre. People who enjoy your first book are more likely to read the next if it is in the same genre.

Choosing Your Genre

You may enjoy reading all sorts of different genres, which can make it difficult to choose only one for your writing. However, your decision can be affected by your goals. Although certain genres are much more popular than others, some have a niche but loyal audience. Think carefully about what you want to achieve with your writing and choose a genre that will best help you to achieve your goals.

Research

Make sure that you do your research on any genres that interest you. In particular, pay attention to the following:

- ○ **Audience size**: Some genres have huge potential audiences, while others are much smaller. If your goal is to reach a large number of readers, choose a genre with a large audience.

- ○ **Competition**: While some genres contain tens of thousands of books, thus making discoverability a challenge, some subgenres have only a few hundred titles in them.

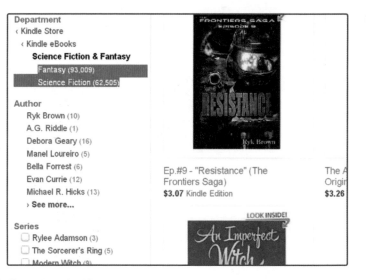

Above: The sci-fi and fantasy genres are highly competitive. There is a large number of books in each category on Amazon.

⊙ **Work:** Some genres, such as fantasy, generally require you to write very long books, while others, such as historical fiction, are very research-intensive. Make sure you are prepared for the added work your chosen genre may entail.

Writing to Market

When doing your research, make sure that you take a look at the most successful books in a genre. Ask yourself: what is it that makes those books popular? Look at the product descriptions, covers and the premises of the stories, and see if you can spot what they have in common. Knowing what works in a particular genre is crucial for writing a successful book, although it may take more than one attempt to get it right.

Writing in Multiple Genres

The great thing about self-publishing is that there are no restrictions to the number of genres you can write in. You can try various ones and see what you are good at. If you write a book in a specific genre that does not sell, or receives negative reviews, you can always write something in a different genre and see if you have more success. Some writers excel in one category but struggle in another. Experiment until you find something that fits your writing.

Above: Stephen King writes in multiple genres, although he is mostly known for horror.

YOUR AUTHOR NAME

In order for readers to identify you, you will need an author name. Many authors use their own name, while others adopt a pseudonym. Whatever you decide, your author name is important for building your brand and platform.

YOUR BRAND

Authors such as Stephen King, J.K. Rowling and James Patterson are household names. When people buy books by these writers, they pretty much know what to expect. This is because these authors have developed their own brand, which is essential for all writers.

Author Name

Your author name serves several purposes:

- **Recognition**: Your name is what readers will use to look for more books by you.

- **Expectation**: When you have developed a brand, readers will come to know what to expect when they pick up books with your name on them.

- **Identification**: Your author name can become synonymous with a certain genre or style of book.

Above: Authors like J.K. Rowling have created their own brand.

Using a Pen Name

The only tool at your disposal to create a brand is your author name. While many writers choose to use their own name, you don't have to, and there are very good reasons to adopt a pseudonym.

- **Famous namesake**: If your name is Stephen King or James Patterson, it is best to adopt a pseudonym in order to avoid confusion with your more established namesakes.

- **Expectations**: Unfortunately, some readers expect certain genres to be written by a particular type of author. Men wishing to write romance may want to consider a female pen name, while women writing military fiction may wish to choose a male name.

- **Common names**: If your name is not very memorable, adopting a pen name may be better than sticking with John Smith or Sue Jones.

- **Personal life**: You may have a professional reputation that could be affected by your writing, such as being a schoolteacher who writes erotica.

- **Genre**: You may wish to write in several genres. Adopting a name for each genre will help you to build up separate platforms, and avoid confusing and frustrating readers' expectations.

Hot Tip

When the Harry Potter stories were published, which were aimed at young boys, Joanne Rowling used her initials, J.K., to hide the fact that she was a woman.

Left: P.D. James and J.K. Rowling adopted initials to hide their genders when they first started writing.

Coming up with a Pen Name

When coming up with a pen name, think about the genre you have chosen and pick a name to suit. If you are writing a hardcore thriller, you may wish to adopt a macho name. Likewise, you may wish to have a soft, feminine name if you are writing romances. However, avoid using a name that sounds too contrived, such as Jack Power or Felicity Valentine.

Using Your Pen Name

It is important to remember that your pen name is simply your brand, not an alter ego. You will still have to pay your taxes under

Above: When dealing with official companies, you should give both your real name and pen name.

your real name and in certain territories, such as the United States, registering for copyright under a pen name can sometimes cause confusion. When dealing with publishers, agents and the Copyright Office, and corresponding with self-publishing platforms, it is best to use your real name with the suffix, 'writing as ...' afterwards.

DEVELOPING YOUR AUTHOR BRAND

Choosing your author name is only the first step to developing a brand. You need to adopt an individual style for the covers of your books so that they become recognizable as being yours (more on this in chapter four). You must also keep in mind that how your author name appears on your books can make a big difference.

Hot Tip

Before settling on your author name, check its availability on social media platforms, such as Facebook and Twitter, as well as seeing if it is available as a website domain; all this will help when it comes to promoting your brand.

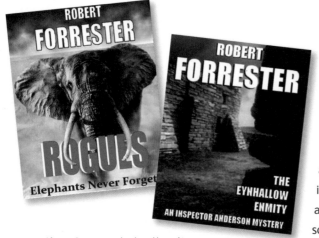

Above: Create an author brand by making your name appear the same way on all your books.

The Cover

Creating an author brand for your books means ensuring that your name appears in a similar way on each of your novels. You should create a design for your author name, which can be used for all of your covers. In addition, if you already have other books available, make sure that your covers include a reference to some of them to attract people who have already read some of your work, such as a tag line at the top that says: 'From the author of ...'

SOFTWARE

The old days of thumping away on a typewriter are thankfully over for writers. However, choosing the right software on which to write your manuscript can make a difference when it comes to converting and formatting your work into the various e-book platforms.

WORD PROCESSORS

With the ability to cut and paste, save, format and spellcheck your work, word processing platforms make writing a novel much easier than when all writers had to use typewriters. For self-publishers, word processing software can do a lot more than just let you draft your book. Many software programs let you write, format and even convert your novel to the various e-book formats, although it can often be a lot better to choose bespoke software systems for each stage of self-publishing. In addition, when it comes to writing your novel, different word processing programs have their pros and cons.

Microsoft Word

By far the most common and widely used word processing program, MS Word is available on both Macs and PCs. Many self-published authors use

Hot Tip

Choose the word processing software that you feel most comfortable with or that is most familiar to you. Writing a novel is difficult enough, without the distraction of having to learn a new program.

Below: Microsoft Word.

Word both to write and format their manuscripts, as most self-publishing platforms, such as Amazon's KDP (Kindle Digital Publishing), Smashwords and Kobo, will automatically convert Word files into the various e-book formats, thus saving you from having to do it. However, in order to use Word effectively, you will need to learn how to use 'Styles' (*see* page 103).

Above: LibreOffice.

Above: Scrivener.

LibreOffice Writer

A free, open-source word processor that is becoming increasingly popular, LibreOffice can handle most word processing files, including .doc (MS Word) and .rtf (rich text format). In addition, you can download extensions to convert documents into ePub files, which is one of the most common e-reader file formats.

Scrivener

Scrivener is fast becoming the software of choice for many fiction writers, as it lets you group documents together, thus enabling you to store notes, research files and other documents along with your manuscript. Scrivener is more of a literary project management tool than just a word processor, as it is designed specifically for writing books. It can also convert files into various e-book formats. Its only main disadvantage is the steep learning curve involved.

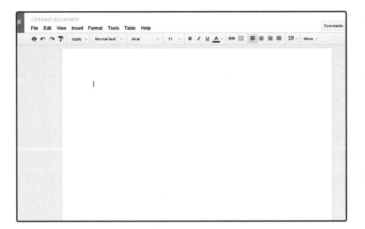

Google Docs

Google Docs lets you write and store your files online. While extremely simple, Google Docs is great for collaborative works, as different users can work on the same project over the internet.

Left: Google Docs.

TEXT EDITORS

In addition to standard word processing software, you may find basic text editors useful. These are ideal for removing Styles and hidden code caused by word processors, which can cause problems when converting files into various e-book formats. Some basic text editors include the following:

○ **WordPad**: A simple word processing tool that comes free with most Windows computers.

○ **Notepad**: A text-only program that is useful for removing all hidden code from word processing software but is not recommended for use when writing a manuscript.

○ **TextEdit**: Similar to WordPad, TextEdit comes free with most Mac computers.

○ **Q10**: A basic word processor and text editor that has all the proofing tools needed to write a manuscript, such as a spellchecker, but none of the formatting and style options.

Hot Tip

No matter which word processing platform you choose, always save your work as .doc or .rtf files, as these formats are more widely accepted than others.

BACKING UP

When you sit down and write your novel, it is not enough just to save your work on your PC or laptop. Work is easily lost. If your hard drive fails, or your laptop is lost or stolen, you can lose many weeks or even months of work. Ensure that you have a reliable system to back up your work and, preferably, use more than one backup method.

Above: To avoid losing work, back it up using methods such as cloud storage system Dropbox.

- **Memory sticks**: You can keep a copy of your work on a memory stick or other removable storage device.

- **Cloud storage**: Systems such as Dropbox, Google Drive and Microsoft SkyDrive are great for backups and can also synchronize files on numerous devices.

- **Hard copies**: Once your novel is finished, it is always a good idea to produce a printed hard copy, just in case you lose the digital one.

- **Second computer**: If you own more than one computer, make sure that you save a copy of your work on each one, just in case.

PUTTING PEN TO PAPER

Finding the time to sit down and write is not always easy, especially if you have family and work commitments, which is why so many people start writing a book but never finish. However, with a little discipline and planning, it is quite possible to get your novel down on paper, no matter how hectic your life is.

WRITING DISCIPLINE

Writing a novel can be exciting and exhilarating, especially when the story is coming together or the characters are developing and seemingly taking on a life of their own. However, at other times, it can be drudgery, which is why all writers need discipline. The only way to finish a novel is to put your backside on a seat and write, but this can be easier said than done.

Finding the Time

Many new authors have to cope with a day job when they write their first novel. In fact, even some established authors still have to hold down a job and write in their spare time. Finding the time to write can be the biggest challenge for a writer, and it usually means making sacrifices.

Early Bird or Night Owl?

The best time to write will depend on the type of person you are and your daily commitments. For example, some people are too exhausted after work to do anything other than sit in front of the TV. For them, getting up early and doing an hour or two before they get to work may be the best way to fit in some writing time each day. On the other hand, other people find mornings a drag and may fare better by spending an hour or two in the evenings on their novel.

Dealing with Distractions

Some people think that they can only write when there is absolute silence and no distractions. However, waiting for such a perfect time to put pen to paper will inevitably mean you'll never finish your book. Learning to cope with distractions is crucial if you ever want to complete your novel.

- **Family**: If you are trying to work with children around you, set aside some time in the day to spend with them and some time to write. If they are at that age when they take naps, take advantage of the peace and quiet then.

- **Procrastination**: It can be all too easy to allow yourself to become distracted. Switch off the TV when you are working and unplug the internet.

- **Socializing**: If you want to finish your novel, you may have to give up those weekends in the pub, or sacrifice some of your favourite TV programmes.

Hot Tip

Every word or sentence you write on your novel is a step closer to finishing it. Even if you can only steal the odd five minutes here and there throughout the day, put some words down. You will be surprised how quickly it all builds up.

MOTIVATION

Novels can range from 50,000 words to over 100,000, and it can be very difficult to keep up the momentum, especially if you can only snatch an hour or two every now and again.

Daily Word Counts

One of the best ways to keep motivated is to work to a daily word count. This can be anything from a couple of hundred words a day to several thousand,

Word Count [?] [X]

Statistics:

Pages	24
Words	4,178
Characters (no spaces)	19,907
Characters (with spaces)	23,885
Paragraphs	204
Lines	603

☐ Include textboxes, footnotes and endnotes

[Close]

Above: Daily word counts can keep you motivated.

depending on how much time you have available. Even if all you can manage each day is 500 words, you can still have a 70,000-word novel completed in just 20 weeks. Double your word count to 1,000 a day and you can have it completed in half that time!

Hot Tip

Each November is NaNoWriMo (National Novel Writing Month). This annual, worldwide competition challenges people to write a 50,000-word novel in a month and can be a great motivational tool to finally getting that novel written.

Keeping a Log

Another great motivational tool is to keep a word-count log. Use a spreadsheet program and enter your word count each day so that you can automatically track your progress and see how far you have come each week.

Writing Days

No matter how busy your life is, you may find that there are entire days – maybe just once a week or once a month – which you can dedicate to writing. Perhaps you have holiday owing at work or you can steal every other Sunday afternoon. These writing days can really help with your progress.

Celebrate Your Targets

Writing a novel is an accomplishment. Select milestones, such as every 20,000 words written or the completion of a first draft, and celebrate them. Treat yourself to a night out or buy yourself a little gift as a means to keep you motivated.

Left: NaNoWriMo is an annual challenge to write a 50,000–word novel during the month of November.

OUTLINES

Some writers cannot pick up a pen until they have outlined every stage of their novel. Other writers do no outlining at all and pull ideas from thin air as they write. It can be difficult to know what is best for you. Although sometimes outlining can stifle creativity and make a story sound contrived, without an outline, it can be all too easy to write yourself into a dead end.

Novel Outline

Scene 1.

A murders B over a debt, but frames C who was having an affair with B

Scene 2.

The police arrive on the scene and arrest C.

Scene 3.

C escapes from prison and embarks to clear their name.

Scene 4.

Aware she could prove her innocence, A hunts down C and tries to kill her.

Above: A novel outline can be useful for planning, but do not stick to it rigidly.

Be Flexible

If you do use an outline, do not stick to it rigidly; instead, be prepared to make changes as your characters and story develop. You may find the ideas you originally had are unworkable as the characters evolve. If you do not have an outline and find yourself stuck, try writing one to see if you can come up with ways to move the story forward.

Hot Tip

Even if you do not write an outline, try to come up with an idea for the ending of a story. Knowing where you are going, even if you are not sure how you will get there, will make your life much easier.

WRITING IN DRAFTS

When you first start writing, it can be very tempting to keep going over the pages that you have written and make changes until they are perfect. However, this is the easiest way to never finish your book. The best way to ensure that you are always moving forward is to write in drafts. How many drafts you will need will depend on how quickly the story comes together and is quite personal to each writer. Some authors write two or three drafts, whereas others write dozens.

The First Draft

The first draft of a novel is the hardest. This is because you are trying to develop characters, create a story arc and come up with plot ideas. Since there is so much to do in a first draft, many writers prefer to ignore their spelling, grammar, punctuation and style, and just get the story down. If you come up with ideas as you write, avoid cycling back. Just make a note so you can make changes in your next draft.

Hot Tip

When writing a first draft, do not be tempted to read back what you have just written. All writers cringe at their first drafts; instead, just carry on and get to the end before rereading it.

Finish What You Start

All writers have feelings of doubt. You may feel that what you are writing is a silly idea or leading nowhere. However, work through these feelings and finish what you start, no matter how poor an idea you think the story is. After you have finished the first draft, put it away for a few weeks and then return to it with fresh eyes – you may be surprised by how good your work actually is.

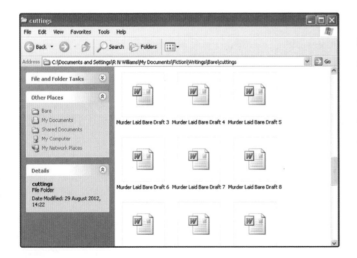

REDRAFTING

Once you have finished your first draft, it is time to start the redrafting process. The purpose of a second, third or fourth draft is not only to hone the actual writing but to make sure the story is as good as it can be. If you have come up with new ideas, you may have to add new sections, delete certain chapters or alter the plot.

Left: It is a good idea to write several drafts of your story rather than keep overwriting the same pages.

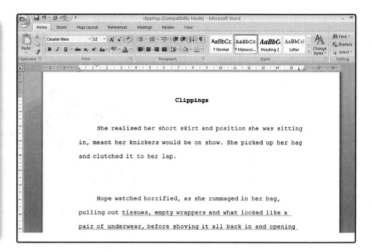

Hot Tip

If you make cuts to your novel, keep everything you take out in a clippings file. You may be able to use these scenes later on, or you may even be able to work them into another book.

Above: A clippings file with text that could be used in later sections or in another novel.

Be Brutal

When you are redrafting, you need to be merciless and take out anything that does not move the story forward or help to develop your characters. Think about books that you have read. Have you ever come across sections that you wanted to skip? Make sure your readers never feel this way: when in doubt, take it out.

REVISING YOUR NOVEL

Once you have your story down pat and you feel it is as good as it can be, it is time to revise your novel. Revision is the process of fine-tuning your sentences and ensuring that your writing is at its best. Do not rush your revision. Although grammar and spellcheckers in word-processing software are useful tools, they are not enough. Read your work aloud, look at each sentence and ask yourself whether you could improve it.

Some Revision Tips

- **Active voice:** Avoid the passive voice where possible. Look for 'to be' verbs (was, were, had been, etc.) and strengthen your sentences.

- **Strong verbs**: Avoid using too many adverbs and adjectives. Try to find strong verbs and descriptive nouns.

- **Dialogue tags**: Remove unnecessary dialogue tags, and try to avoid using anything other than he/she said, such as he grumbled, or she hissed.

- **Beta readers**: Give your novel to other readers to look through. A fresh set of eyes may spot things in the story that you've missed.

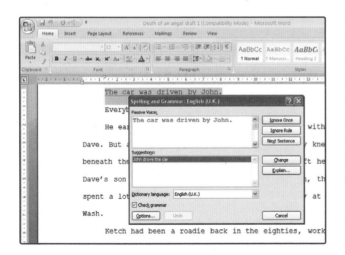

Above: Grammar and spell check your manuscript.

Knowing When It Is Finished

It can be very difficult to know when your book is finished. No novel can ever be perfect, and no matter how many times you revise it, you will always find things that you want to change. Too much redrafting can ruin a novel and you may find that you start putting things back in which you had previously taken out. Be disciplined and know when to say 'enough is enough'. Novels are never really finished, merely set free.

CREATING A PROFESSIONAL MANUSCRIPT

Once you have finished your novel, you may need to find help in order to ensure that it is of the highest possible quality. For this, you will need to look for an editor, which means presenting your manuscript in a professional way.

FORMATTING YOUR MANUSCRIPT

When you write your novel, it doesn't really matter what fonts, line spacing or formatting you use. However, if you are sending your work to an editor, you will need to present it in a way that is easy to work with. You also need to ensure that it is in a form which is easy to convert into an e-book.

Chapters

Chapters are natural breaks in the text that allow readers a resting point, as well as providing a clear indication of when there is a change of scene, time or location in the story. There are no set rules as to the size of a chapter, although

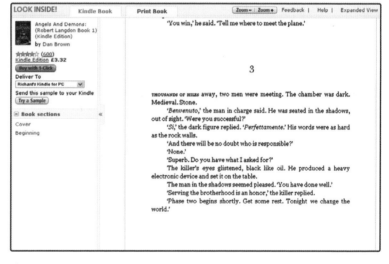

Above: Chapter lengths can vary, and some can even be merely a paragraph in length.

genre can have some influence. Some thriller writers start a new chapter every two or three pages, while other novels have chapters that are 15–20 pages long.

Creating Chapters in Your Manuscript

1. Count the number of pages in your manuscript and divide that by the number of chapters you want in the book; this will give you an approximate number of pages per chapter.

Step 3: Insert a page break at the end of a chapter.

2. Identify natural breaks in the text around each approximate chapter length. It does not matter if some chapters are longer than others.

3. Insert a page break at the end of each chapter (Ctrl/Command Enter on most word processors).

4. On the next page, drop down a few lines, and write 'Chapter' and the chapter number; centre it if you wish.

Step 4: Write 'Chapter' and the chapter number.

Scene Breaks

As well as chapters, you may find that you have natural breaks in the story, such as when you switch point of view or move to a new location. Leave two spaces between each scene to help identify these breaks.

Hot Tip

If you include a hash (#) at the end of a scene break, it will make them easier to spot when they end up at the bottom of a page; it will also help when it comes to formatting your manuscript as an e-book.

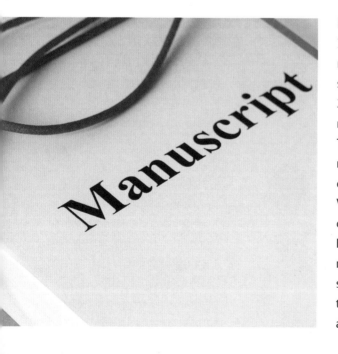

bucket, dripping water on her head and drank. It stared at her for a moment, its beady black eyes unblinking. Then it raised its trunk and bellowed. The shrill noise forced Jeta to cover her ears with her hands.

Finally, she managed a scream.

But only briefly because the elephant lifted its huge leg and brought it down, silencing her forever.

#

Winters in Mayfair dated back to 1847 when Sir Henry Winters, a colonel in the 33rd Regiment of Foot, was kicked

Above: A hash symbol clearly indicates a scene break.

Laying Out Your Manuscript

In the old days, professional manuscripts needed to be double-spaced, to have one-inch margins and 25 lines to a page, and composed in a mono-space font, such as Courier. This was to ensure that editors had room to make notes and could calculate word counts accurately. Word processors have made these conventions largely obsolete. However, make sure that you use a readable font – preferably one with a serif, such as Times New Roman – and that the margins are wide enough for an editor to add comments.

FINDING AN EDITOR

No matter how carefully you revise your manuscript, you will not spot every error. All authors, whether traditionally or self-published, require some editing. For self-publishers, professional editing can be costly, but it is worth the money. A professional editor does more than just fix typos and spelling mistakes. In fact, there are different types of editor.

Hot Tip

If you cannot afford a professional editor, ask friends to proofread your manuscript for errors and use a number of beta readers to give you feedback on the story.

- **Content editing**: A content editor will provide feedback on your entire manuscript, offering suggestions to improve the story, spotting holes in the plot and identifying weaknesses in the novel.

- **Line and copy-editing**: These editors go over your sentences, spotting errors in grammar, spelling and punctuation, as well as offering suggestions to improve style and syntax.

- **Proofreaders**: In publishing, proofreaders are there to check that the proofs that come back from the printer match the edited manuscript. However, among self-publishers, proofreading has come to mean somebody who offers basic copy-editing to spot typos and errors.

Using a Professional

You can find professional freelance editors on the internet, but make sure you do your research. Speak to other writers on self-publishing forums and ask who they use. It is important to choose an editor who has experience in editing books in your genre; also, ensure that you are clear about what you want. If you just need copy-editing, make sure that your editor knows this upfront and you have agreed a fee before they start.

ONLINE EDITING

It is normally not necessary to send a hard copy of your manuscript off to an editor these days, as most of them will edit your manuscript using an electronic copy. You may find that the majority of editors prefer to use MS Word because of its simple-to-use 'Review' and 'Tracking' capabilities.

Tracking Changes

Word processors such as MS Word can track the changes made on a manuscript, which makes editing simple. This is done in the Review pane, under the Track Changes icon.

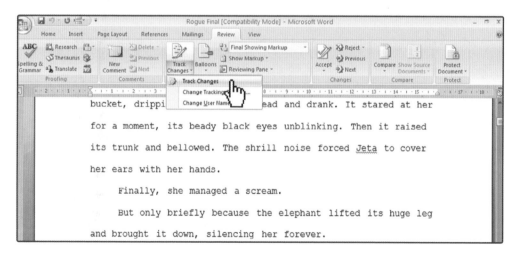

Above: Some word processors allow you to track the changes made to a manuscript.

○ Changes made by an editor will appear in a different colour to your normal text.

Above: Changes made by an editor will be in a different colour.

○ Deleted words and punctuation will have a score through them, while added words will be underlined.

○ In order to accept or decline a change made by an editor, right-click it and select 'Accept Change' or 'Reject change'.

Above: Select 'Accept Change' if you agree with the editor's revision.

Hot Tip

Each user on a document is assigned a different colour when you are tracking changes. This enables you to make your own revisions and then send them back to the editor for approval.

Comments

Using the Review pane on MS Word, an editor is also able to add comments to a manuscript. When an editor adds a comment, the relevant text is highlighted and a comment balloon will appear in the right-hand margin. You can delete the comments by right-clicking them once you have read them.

Above: Comment balloons appear in the right-hand margin of an MS Word document.

Final Check

Even the best editors make mistakes. Once you have received your edited manuscript back and made any recommended changes, it is always a good idea to give it one final read-through. Make sure you double-check for common errors.

- **Omitted or repeated words**: It is very easy to miss repetitions and omissions of small words, such as a, is, in or the.

- **Homophone errors**: Words that sound the same but are spelled differently are easy to miss, such as draw/drawer, your/you're, duel/dual.

- **Apostrophes**: Double-check possessives and contractions to ensure the correct use of apostrophes, such as its/it's, lets/let's and student's/students' (plural).

LECTRONIC BOOK

Chapter 3

Lorem ipsum dolor sit amet, consectetur adipiscing elit. Nunc rutrum dolor ut convallis tempor. Praesent lacinia turpis felis, et adipiscing metus adipiscing nec. Maecenas vitae urna sem. Pellentesque habitant morbi tristique senectus et netus et malesuada fames ac turpis egestas. Suspendisse tempus augue quis condimentum pharetra. Quisque pharetra turpis vel tempus varius. Curabitur faucibus, quam at venenatis tincidunt, ante nibh pretium tellus, eu eleifend arcu turpis quis leo. Aliquam ut est quis magna tristique varius. Praesent sed ligula massa. In venenatis dui vitae auctor vestibulum. Lorem ipsum dolor sit amet, consectetur adipiscing elit. Nunc rutrum dolor ut convallis tempor. Praesent lacinia turpis felis, et adipiscing metus adipiscing nec. Maecenas vitae urna sem. Pellentesque habitant morbi tristique senectus et netus et malesuada fames ac turpis egestas. Suspendisse tempus augue quis condimentum pharetra. Quisque pharetra turpis vel tempus varius. Curabitur faucibus, quam at

CREATING YOUR DIGITAL PRODUCT

DEVICES

Before you can turn your manuscript into an e-book, it is a good idea to understand the different types of e-reading devices, so that you know how they work and how they present your work to readers.

E-BOOK READING

When you convert your novel into an e-book, you are converting it into a digital file. People can read an e-book file on a specific e-reading device, such as a Kindle, Nook or Kobo, on a tablet computer or smartphone (iPhone, Android, BlackBerry, etc.), or on a computer using an app. These devices and apps present e-books in a similar way to a printed book, with pages that a reader can flick through, albeit using a touchscreen or button. E-book files also contain a digital version of your book cover. However, an e-book does differ to a printed book in several significant ways.

- **Fonts**: E-readers use their own fonts so, unlike a printed book, when you format an e-book, you cannot choose how your words will look on the page.

- **Text size**: Readers can adjust the size of text on an e-reader, which means that the number of words on a page will differ depending on how big or small a size the user has selected.

- **Page numbers**: Since readers can adjust fonts and text sizes, page numbers become irrelevant, and the same book may have a different number of pages, depending on the device and the reader's preferences.

Hot Tip
Most e-reading apps for smartphones, computers and tablets are free to download from the various e-reader manufacturers.

Using Reading Devices
While people can read an e-book on almost any digital device, from e-readers and tablets to smartphones, computers and netbooks, the user experience can differ. Reading on a smartphone, for instance, means that a page will only have a few words on it in order to maintain decent text size, while reading on a laptop or computer is less comfortable than holding a tablet or e-reader in your hands.

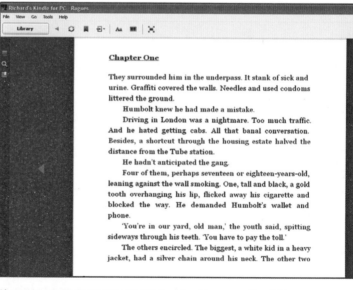

Above: Using the Kindle app on a computer allows for a bigger screen, though it is a less comfortable experience than a tablet or phone.

Multi-device Support

An interesting aspect to e-books is that, thanks to apps, readers can download a book from a particular e-book vendor and read it on a rival e-book publisher's device. For instance, you can download a Kindle book from Amazon and read it on an iPad, despite the iPad being an Apple product.

Advantages of E-books

E-books have numerous advantages over printed books:

- **Storage**: You can store hundreds or even thousands of books on your tablet or e-reading device, making them great for travelling.

- **Adjustable text size**: Having the ability to increase text size is great for people who struggle with small print.

- **Cloud**: You can keep all your e-books online, so you'll be able to download and read them anywhere.

- **Speed and convenience**: You can buy and download books using your computer, smartphone or tablet, and then read them instantly.

- **Price**: Without the same production costs, you can price an e-book much lower than a printed copy.

Above: The price of an e-book is much cheaper than the print version.

Disadvantages of E-books

While e-books offer many advantages over printed books, they are in no way perfect.

- **Initial cost**: The price of an e-reader or tablet can be high, especially for people who only read one or two books a year.

- **Gifts**: You cannot wrap up an e-book and give it as a gift to a friend or family member (although you can still send a digital file as a gift).

- **Eyestrain**: Some tablets and e-readers can strain the eyes.

- **Tactile**: E-readers do not offer the same tactile experience as flicking through the pages of a book.

- **Borrow**: You cannot lend or swap an e-book file with somebody else.

- **Navigation**: Without page numbers, it can be difficult for book clubs and teachers to refer to certain passages. Flicking back and forth can also be cumbersome.

- **Control**: Authors and publishers have little or no control over how a book looks on the screen, due to adjustable fonts and sizes.

- **Piracy**: E-books are easily copied and distributed on the internet.

Hot Tip

In order to aid navigation, you can include a table of contents at the beginning of your book, which contains links to the different chapters.

Above: The contents page at the beginning of an e-book links to the different chapters.

E-book Compatibility

The fact that there are so many different types of e-reading devices poses a challenge for self-published authors. An e-book needs to be viewable on all these devices, from large tablets, with hundreds of words to a page, to a smartphone, where only one or two paragraphs are visible at once. The number of different software platforms used by e-readers compounds this problem, and it is quite common to format an e-book that looks perfect on one device only for it to appear messy on a different one.

E-READING SOFTWARE

E-readers use a number of different software platforms, most of which operate in a similar way. When you convert a file into an e-book, you are essentially converting it into HTML (HyperText Markup Language). This is the language of the internet, and it can only handle basic text. This means that, depending on the e-reading software platform, you may run into problems when using such things as smart quotes or unusual symbols in your work.

File Formats

While numerous different electronic book formats exist, two main platforms are now ubiquitous:

Above: A passage in a book as it appears on a tablet.

Above: The same passage as it appears on a Kindle.

Above: The same passage as it appears on an iPhone.

- **ePub:** The publishing industry's standard e-book format.

- **Mobipocket:** Amazon's own e-book file system that, although based on ePub, is specially adapted for Amazon's devices and apps.

ePub

As the industry standard, ePub is an open file format. This means that any new or existing manufacturer of e-readers or apps can use it. Nearly all stores, other than Amazon, sell e-book files in ePub. As a file format, it allows for more formatting than Mobipocket, including such things as drop caps and text that can flow around images.

> ## Hot Tip
> The Nook, Sony Reader, Kobo and most e-reading apps now all read ePub files (.epub), while Mobi files (.Mobi or .azw) are restricted to Amazon's Kindles and apps.

Mobipocket

Amazon's Mobipocket (also known as just Mobi) is specifically designed for use on Kindle devices. Although most of these newer Amazon devices read ePub formats too, Amazon only sells Mobi files. Its main advantage is that many people find it easier and simpler to convert a file to Mobi than to its rival ePub.

Above: ePub files can be read by most e–reading apps, whereas Mobi files are restricted to Amazon.

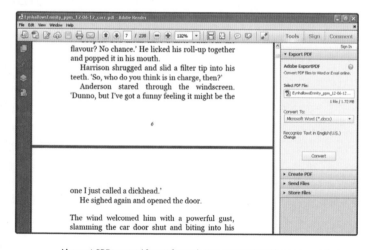

Above: A PDF is a good format for reading on a computer without an e–reading app.

Other File Formats

There are other file formats that are worth considering when you convert your novel, depending on where you plan to sell your book.

- **HTML**: Designed for reading in a web browser, it is worth considering if you plan to serialize a novel on a blog or website.

- **PDF**: Good for printing or for reading on a computer that does not have an e-reading app.

- **RTF**: Readable on most word processors or text editors.

- **LRF**: Used by older models of the Sony Reader, which did not support ePub at the time.

- **Palm Doc (PDB)**: Designed for Palm reading devices.

LICENSING

Unlike printed books, e-books are licensed rather than sold, because an e-book file is software and not a physical item. This means that readers never actually own their e-books, but are licensed to read and store them on their devices. While in reality this does not make much of a difference to the reading experience, it does mean that people are not able to copy, sell, lend or distribute an e-book file without permission.

DRM

In order to protect e-books from piracy, a system called Digital Rights Management (DRM) is used. This essentially locks an e-book file, preventing it from being copied or passed on to anybody other than the rights holder. The various e-book vendors offer self-publishers the choice to implement DRM on their e-books. While it can prevent your work from being unlawfully copied, DRM also has its disadvantages.

- **Limited**: DRM files are often limited to a certain number of devices that a user can view them on, such as one computer and one e-reader.

- **Restrictive**: DRM prevents readers from converting their e-books into other files for reading on different devices.

- **Ineffective**: Determined software pirates have ways to unlock DRM.

Tax

Another aspect of e-books that differs from printed books is that they are taxable in some countries. In the EU, e-books are subject to VAT, which ranges from five to 20 per cent, depending on the country.

Hot Tip

Vendors, such as Amazon, are based in non–UK EU territories, so when you sell e-books through them, they are subject to three per cent VAT rather than 20 per cent, though this may change soon.

E-READING DEVICES

E-books are most commonly read on dedicated e-readers or tablets. This is probably because these devices more closely replicate the feeling of reading a printed book, compared to the small size of a smartphone, or the cumbersome nature of a computer, laptop or netbook. However, e-readers and tablets each use different technologies.

E-ink

Dedicated e-readers, such as Nook, Kindle, Kobo and Sony Reader, use e-ink screens, as opposed to tablets, which use LCD (liquid crystal displays). E-ink more closely resembles printed text on paper, which gives readers several advantages over tablets.

- **No eyestrain:** E-ink is just like reading print, so readers do not suffer eyestrain.

  - **Battery life:** Once a new page loads, an e-ink screen requires no more power, so e-readers can go weeks without needing a recharge.

Left: E-ink readers like the Kindle DX give an experience more like reading printed paper.

- **Direct sunlight**: As it resembles paper and ink, you can use an e-reader in direct sunlight without suffering glare.

- **Lighter**: E-readers tend to be much lighter than tablets and therefore are more comfortable to hold for prolonged periods.

Tablets

The big advantage that tablets (Kindle Fire, iPad, Samsung Galaxy, Google Nexus, B&N Nook HD, etc.) have over dedicated e-readers is that they are multifunctional. This means that not only can you read e-books on them, but you can also surf the internet, send emails, play games and watch videos. Thanks to this, more people are opting for tablets than dedicated e-readers, and they have other advantages too:

- **Colour**: Tablets have full-colour screens, unlike e-readers, which are black and white.

- **Backlight**: While you can now get e-readers with built-in lights, the LCD screens on tablets can be used day or night.

Above: Unlike e-readers, tablets have full-colour screens.

- **Resolution**: Tablets have much better display resolution.

- **Speed**: The refresh rate on a tablet is much quicker when reading an e-book compared to an e-reader, which often has an annoying pause before the page is turned.

Hot Tip
Make sure your e-book cover looks as good in black and white as it does in colour, as you never know what sort of device somebody will be using.

SELF-PUBLISHING PLATFORMS

As a self-publisher, you will find numerous websites where you can upload your e-book and sell directly to readers. We will go into more detail about different options for distributing your e-book in chapters five and six, but it is worth knowing which vendors dominate the e-book market and the distinct advantages they offer the indie publisher.

Above: Thousands of new books are uploaded to Amazon every week through Kindle Direct Publishing.

AMAZON

Claiming to have a market share of up to 80 per cent, Amazon is by far the biggest e-book retailer. Their self-publishing platform, KDP (Kindle Direct Publishing), is the most popular, and tens of thousands of new books are uploaded onto Amazon through KDP each week. While this means there is a lot of competition, Amazon makes it easy to market and reach readers.

Amazon's KDP Program

The advantages of enrolling in KDP include the following:

○ **Audience:** Over 100 million customers shop on Amazon each month, and their Kindles are the most popular e-readers on the market, with tens of millions of people owning one.

Hot Tip

If you have already shopped at Amazon, you can use your account details to enrol in KDP. Just click the 'Independently Publish with Us' link at the bottom of their homepage.

- **Reach:** When you upload to KDP, your e-book can be available on all of Amazon's websites, including the US, UK, France, Germany, Mexico, Brazil, Japan, India, Spain, Italy, Canada and Australia.

- **Uploading:** Uploading to KDP is incredibly easy. You can upload your book as a Word file (.doc) or HTML, or you can upload Mobi or ePub files.

- **Marketing tools:** Amazon offers indie publishers all sorts of ways to promote their books, from allowing giveaways and discounts to targeting readers who have read similar titles.

APPLE

While Apple has long dominated the MP3 market, it has failed to replicate that success with e-books. However, the iBookstore is still very popular, and uploading to Apple means that you will be able to reach the millions of iTunes users who regularly shop at the Apple Store.

Above: The Apple iBookstore.

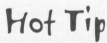

Above: Kobo is particularly popular in Canada and the UK.

KOBO

The leading e-book retailer in Canada, Kobo is also popular in the UK and therefore uploading your e-book there will allow you to reach all of its customers. Moreover, they also supply e-books to major high-street chains, including WH Smith.

NOOK STORE

America's leading bookstore chain, Barnes & Noble, also produce the Nook e-reader. While nowhere near as popular as the Kindle, the Nook still has many users, especially in the United States, so it is worth considering for any self-publisher wanting to maximize their reach in the US.

SMASHWORDS

Although they have their own retail store, the main advantage of uploading your e-book to Smashwords is that they act as an aggregator and will distribute your book in multiple formats to all the main e-book retailers (other than Amazon).

Hot Tip

By uploading to an aggregator service, such as Smashwords, you can distribute your book to most of the major e-book retailers all at once, without having to upload your e-book to each vendor individually.

FORMATTING FOR E-BOOK PLATFORMS

Before you can upload your e-book to any retailers and distributors, you need to ensure that you have formatted your manuscript for e-book conversion. You can choose whether to convert your manuscript to e-book files yourself or upload it directly to e-book retailers.

PREPARING YOUR MANUSCRIPT

Many features of a manuscript are often unnecessary when it comes to converting your work into an e-book file. Some aspects can even cause problems in the conversion process if you do not remove them.

- **Page numbers**: As e-books do not use page numbers, you should remove them from your manuscript.

- **Headers and footers**: These can cause issues, so remove them (you can delete them in the Insert menu in MS Word).

Above: Headers and footers can cause problems, so it is best to remove them.

- **Fonts**: As e-readers and apps select their own fonts, just use a single one for your entire document. In order to do this, simply select all (Ctrl + A) and choose one font from the drop-down menu.

Italics and Bold

Both ePub and Mobi files can handle italics and bold text. However, if you have underlined words in your manuscript to indicate italics (a common publishing practice), then ensure that you remove this, otherwise it will appear in the e-book file. The easiest way to do this is to select all the text in your manuscript (Ctrl + A), then click the underline button (or Ctrl + U) twice to underline everything first and then take the underline away.

Hot Tip

Make sure you save a copy of your original manuscript before making changes for e-book conversion, as you may not be able to undo them.

Editing Notes

Double-check that you have removed any notes, comments and annotations left by your editor. If you forget to remove these, you may find they appear in your e-book or cause problems when you are formatting to ePub or Mobi.

Formatting

If you have included special formatting, such as drop caps, in your manuscript, you may find this does not convert well using the conversion platforms used by self-publishing platforms. If the special formatting is definitely required, you may find that you have to use a program such as InDesign or Calibre to convert your file into an e-book, rather than uploading your word processor file directly.

Special Characters and Smart Quotes

Using special characters, such as dollar signs ($), can cause problems in e-book files, so use the find-and-replace function to remove them if possible, otherwise you will have to embed them using a program such as InDesign.

Smart Quotes

Smart (curly) quotes also cause problems, especially with ePub, but they can be complicated to remove.

1. In MS Word, go into the Word Options menu and select Proofing.

2. Click on AutoCorrect Options. Under the AutoFormat tab, unclick where it says: "'Straight quotes' with "smart quotes"'. Do the same in the AutoFormat As You Type tab.

3. Go back into your document. Select and copy an opening smart quote.

4. Open the Find and Replace menu (Ctrl + F). Paste the smart quote into the 'Find what' pane and then

Step 2: Unclick the option to replace straight quotes with smart.

Step 4: Paste a smart quote into the 'Find what' pane and type a quote mark into the 'Replace with' pane.

type a quote mark, which should now be straight, in the 'Replace with' pane.

5.   Click Replace All.

6.   Repeat the process for closing quote marks and apostrophes.

Hot Tip

Mobi files permit smart quotes, whereas ePub files do not, so if you want to include them in your Kindle version, convert to Mobi first and then remove them before converting to ePub.

COPYRIGHT AND TITLE PAGE

All e-books should have a title page that includes your author name. In addition, you should include a copyright page. This does not need to be lengthy, but should include the name of the copyright owner (the author), the edition and publication date. You can also include the relevant passage of law that governs copyright, and a notice that it is a work of fiction. While these are not strictly necessary, they do make your book look more professional.

Above: The copyright page should include the name of the author, the edition and the publication date.

Other Works and Author Biography

If you have other books out or due for release, it is worthwhile including a brief description, as well as links to them, in your e-book. However, vendors will not accept links to a rival company, so you may have to do several versions. Readers also like to know a little bit about an author, so include a short biography.

FORMATTING AND CONVERSION: THE EASY WAY

There are numerous ways to convert your file into an e-book, but perhaps the simplest one is to format your document using your word processor and then upload it directly to the various self-publishing platforms. While most word processors are capable of this, MS Word is probably the easiest to use, although you do need to know how to use Styles.

USING STYLES

Word processors often leave a lot of hidden code lying around, which can cause problems when converting to an e-book. The best way to prevent this problem is to format everything using Styles. These are set formats that you can use to ensure that your entire document is formatted the same way throughout. You will find them in the Home pane in MS Word, but you will need to modify a Style to suit your needs. For your main document, it is best to modify the Style labelled Normal, as this is the default Style to which Word will revert if you accidentally miss a section.

Step 1: Click Modify.

Step 3: Select Paragraph from the Format tab.

Step 5: Select the indent size for the first line.

Modifying Styles in MS Word

1. Right-click the Style you want to edit and click Modify.

2. Choose a font and its size, and then click the Justify button, which will ensure that you have a neat right-hand side rather than a raggedy edge.

3. Click the Format tab at the bottom of the menu and select Paragraph.

4. In the Paragraph menu, choose your line spacing (1.5 is good for e-books).

5. Under Indentation, select 'First line' in the Special drop-down menu. Where it says By, select an amount (0.5 in/1.25 cm is recommended for e-books).

6. Click OK to return to the Styles menu and then click OK to save your changes.

Applying Your Style

While you may want certain aspects of your book in a different Style, such as chapter headings, it is best to apply your Style to the entire document and then adjust the other aspects later.

In order to apply, simply select all (Ctrl + A) and click your modified Style in the Styles box.

Above: Highlight everything, then click the relevant Styles box.

Other Styles

You may want to modify another couple of Styles for different features and pages in your e-book:

- **Chapter headings:** These can be in bold, larger text, centred and underlined if you wish.

- **Copyright page:** Keep your copyright notice in small print, such as size 8. You should also centre it.

> ## Hot Tip
> For a professional-looking book, remove the indent on the first line of a chapter or scene. If you have left marks between scene breaks, use the Find menu to search for them.

Adding Links

You can add links using the Hyperlink button on the Insert pane in MS Word. These can be links to external websites, such as where to buy your other titles, or actual locations in the book. Some authors include a table of contents, which lists all the chapter numbers and includes a link to each one.

VENDOR CONVERSION

Most e-book vendors will accept your document as a Word file (.doc) and do the conversion to e-book for you. For most self-publishers, this is the easiest and preferred option, although with some vendors, it is not without its difficulties.

Amazon

Uploading your .doc file to Amazon's KDP platform is fairly simple and rarely problematic. Make sure you take advantage of the previewer to see how your e-book will look on the various different platforms. If you run into problems, Amazon.com has its own Getting Started guide that can help.

Meatgrinder

In order to reach as many vendors as possible, most self-publishers take advantage of Smashwords' aggregator service. This platform will convert your document into various different formats and will also create a table of contents for you. However, their uploading platform, known as Meatgrinder, is notoriously problematic and many authors find they run into trouble.

> ## Hot Tip
> Smashwords will only accept your document file if it contains the words 'Smashwords Edition' next to the copyright notice.

NUCLEAR OPTION

If you run into formatting issues using Meatgrinder or any other e-book platform, as a last resort, you can copy and paste your entire document into a text editor such as Windows Notepad. This will remove all styles and formatting, thus allowing you to start again. This has been coined 'the nuclear option' and is only recommended if you cannot rectify formatting issues in any other way.

HTML

Since e-books use markup language, it can often create fewer problems with vendor conversion if you convert your .doc file into a web page file before uploading it. This makes it easier to spot potential problems and fine-tune any formatting issues before uploading your file.

1. Once you have formatted your manuscript, click Options in Word and select Save As.

2. Select Web Page, filtered in the Save as type menu.

3. Click Save.

4. Your file will now be converted into an HTML file. You can continue to edit this in Word and make changes before uploading it to the various e-book vendors.

Step 2: Select Web Page, filtered.

CREATING YOUR OWN E-BOOK FILES

Another solution to formatting issues is to create your own e-book files. This also gives you more freedom to make your e-book look how you want it to. However, for this, you will first need some e-book management software.

CALIBRE

Calibre is one of the most common and easy-to-use e-book management software systems available. It is free to download, and you can upload and convert all sorts of files. If you have already converted your document into a Kindle file, you can convert this into an ePub, or you can choose to create your own Mobi and ePub files from your Word document.

Calibre is available at www.calibre-ebook.com. You will find versions for Windows, Linux and OS X. In order to use it, select the relevant operating system, download and install on your machine.

Above: Calibre is a free and easy-to-use e-book management software system.

Hot Tip

Calibre also includes an e-book viewer that can read all e-book formats. This can be useful for checking e-book files that have been converted on vendor platforms.

Using Calibre

Once you have prepared your manuscript (removed page numbers, headers, etc.), you can upload it to Calibre and prepare it for conversion.

1. Click Add Books, select the file you want to convert and click Open.

2. Highlight the file in the main window and then click Edit Metadata.

3. Fill in your book's details. Make sure you include: Title, Author, Series (if it is part of a series), Tags (more on these in the next chapter), Publisher (if you are using a publisher name) and Comments (for your product information; more on this in the next chapter too).

4. You can upload a cover by clicking Browse, although most vendors expect you to upload covers separately. Then click OK.

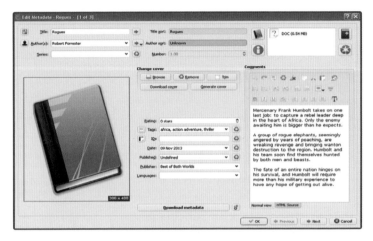

Step 3: Fill in the various details for your book.

Select Your E-book Format

1. After you have entered your metadata, click the Convert Books button to bring up the conversion menu.

2. Select Zip as Input Format and whatever e-book format you want in the Output Format menu.

Adjustment Menus

Click the Conversion button to bring up the Conversion menu. This includes various features to help you format your e-book:

Step 1: To select your e-book format, first bring up the Conversion menu.

○ **Look & Feel:** Lets you make basic format adjustments. You may want to leave this, unless your converted file does not look the way you want it to.

○ **Structure Detection:** Calibre can automatically identify your chapter headings. You can also choose how they look.

○ **Table of Contents:** You can adjust your table of contents or allow Calibre to generate it automatically.

○ **Page Setup:** You can adjust margins and select formatting for specific devices and models of e-reader.

○ **Heuristic Processing:** Has some useful features, such as the ability to remove unnecessary hyphens.

○ **Search & Replace:** Used for last-minute editing.

Hot Tip

Select Smarten Punctuation in the Look & Feel menu to ensure that your quotes, dashes and other punctuation are correct, just in case you've missed any smart quotes.

Conversion

Once you hit OK, Calibre will convert your file into your chosen e-book format. Make sure you check it in the e-book viewer, and repeat the process if you need to make changes.

MOBI TO ePUB CONVERSION

Due to the ease with which Amazon KDP converts .doc files into Mobi format, and the difficulty ePub conversion causes in platforms such as Smashwords, many self-publishers opt to use KDP to create their Mobi file and Calibre to create ePubs.

1. Download your Mobi file from KDP and upload it to Calibre.

2. Make adjustments
    to your metadata.
    Make sure you
    include a product
    description, which
    Amazon Mobi
    files do not contain.

3. Choose ePub as your
    output file in the
    Conversion menu

Step 3: Select ePub as your output file.

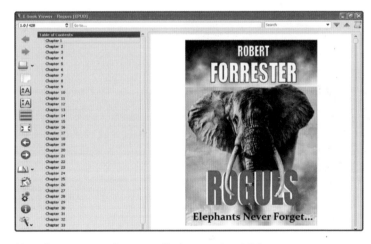

4. Check the 'Force use
    of auto-generated
    Table of Contents' in the
    Table of Contents menu.

5. Hit OK to convert.

6. In order to convert
    from ePub to Mobi,
    simply swap around the
    input and output files.

Above: You can automatically create a table of contents through Calibre.

Hot Tip

Amazon's KDP platform does not generate a table of contents, but if
you upload your Mobi file to Calibre and choose Mobi as the output file,
you can automatically create one.

ADVANCED FORMATTING

For most novels, using a word processing program such as Word and an e-book management tool like Calibre is all you need to create a professional-looking book. However, some books have specific formatting requirements. A book containing a lot of illustrations, for instance, may be extremely difficult to get right using Word or Calibre, and the same is true for e-books with special formatting, such as epistolary novels, featuring letters or diary entries.

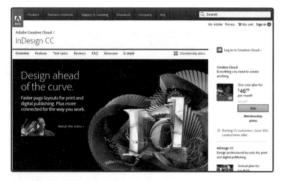

Above: InDesign is the leading industry standard publishing platform.

Above: QuarkXPress is another popular publishing program.

DESKTOP PUBLISHING SOFTWARE

For books that require more advanced formatting, it may be necessary to use desktop publishing software. Various programs are around, but most do involve quite a steep learning curve.

- **InDesign:** The leading and industry-standard publishing platform. The latest version allows for direct ePub conversion, but it does come with a fairly steep price tag.

- **PagePlus:** Similar to InDesign in functionality, but quite a bit cheaper.

- **QuarkXPress:** Another fully functional desktop publishing system.

○ **Scribus**: A free, open-source platform that is ideal for anybody who cannot afford the price tag of commercial software.

Creating an ePub in InDesign

InDesign allows you to insert images into your e-book, position the text exactly how you wish and embed fonts, so that e-readers will display them precisely as they appear in InDesign. After you have designed your e-book, converting a document into an ePub file is fairly simple.

1. Open your document, click File, then Save As and name the book file.

> ## Hot Tip
> You can find a free plug-in for Adobe InDesign on the Amazon website, which allows you to export to Kindle directly.

2. Select Choose File, then Document Setup. In the setup window, select Digital Publishing from the Intent drop-down menu. Choose your page size and orientation, then click OK and save the file.

Step 3: Choose Export for from the File menu.

3. Select File and Export for Digital editions.

4. Choose your options for embedding fonts, then make adjustments in the General, Images and Contents options to suit your requirements.

5. Click Export to create your ePub file.

Step 4: Make adjustments to the options according to your own requirements.

APPLE STORE

Apple has also released its own formatting program called iBooks Author, which is free in the Apple App Store and makes uploading and formatting e-books for Apple devices extremely simple. However, you do need an Apple computer to upload to the Apple Store.

Using iBooks Author

One of the big advantages of iBooks Author is its ease of use. The program has 15 built-in templates and an online tutorial that provides all the step-by-step information you need to create and format your book. It also has plenty of useful features:

- **Import**: You can import your text files directly from Word or other word processing programs.

- **Images**: iBooks Author allows you to import and position all sorts of image files.

- **Multimedia**: You can include a video in your e-book, that plays when somebody first opens the book, which is a great way to showcase your work.

- **Export**: You can export directly to the iBook Store, as well as creating versions for other e-book devices, such as Amazon's Kindle.

Above: iBooks Author is easy to use, as it offers templates and an online tutorial.

OTHER FORMATTING SOLUTIONS

While many self-publishers learn to format their own books, not everybody is comfortable with the process or feels confident about handling their own e-book formatting and conversion. A simple option for self-publishers in this position is to hire third-party help. As with hiring an editor, you can find plenty of people on the internet (and on self-publishing forums) offering formatting services. However, ensure you research their services carefully and ask other authors for recommendations.

Online Services

Some popular services for e-book production include BookBaby.com, Booktango.com and Lulu.com. As well as formatting and conversion, these websites offer some marketing and promotional services. They also provide a distribution service, which is similar to Smashwords, for getting your e-book to all the main vendors.

Hot Tip

If you use a third-party formatter, ensure that you get the formatted word processor files as well as any e-books they have created; you can use these as a template to format your next book yourself.

Above: Bookbaby.com offers marketing and distribution services.

FORMATTING FOR PRINT

Print-on-demand services, such as CreateSpace, Lulu and Lightning Source, allow you to create and distribute printed books through all the major online book retailers. However, creating a printed book provides a bigger challenge for self-publishers than e-book formatting.

Trim Size

Before you can begin formatting your printed book, you need to decide on a book size, known as the 'trim'. Books can range in trim size, but most paperbacks are 5 x 8 in (12.7 x 20.32 cm).

Adjusting Your Manuscript

If you have already formatted your Word file for e-book conversion, you can use this file as a basis for your print book, but first you have to adjust the page size.

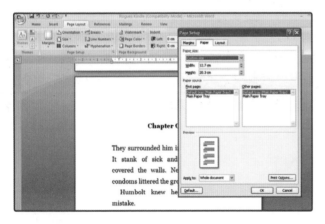

Step 1: Click Size.

Step 2: If necessary, manually create your page size.

1.   Open your document and select the Page Layout tab at the top of the page, then click Size.

2.   Search for your intended book size in the drop-down menu. If it is not there, click More Paper Sizes, enter your book's trim size and click OK.

3.   Your manuscript should now be shrunk to your book size.

Adjusting Margins

Printed books require margins on the side, on the top and bottom, and one in the middle, known as a gutter (the left side on odd pages and the right side on even pages).

1.   Click Margins in the Page Layout menu.

2. Select Custom Margins.

3. Adjust your margins and gutter.
    It is best to allow 0.75 in (1.9 cm)
    for the gutter, 0.5 in (1.27 cm)
    for the right-hand margin, zero
    for the left-hand margin and 1 in
    (2.54 cm) for the top and
    bottom margins.

4. Click OK.

Page Numbers

Insert page numbers in the header or
footer using the Page Number button
in the Insert menu. Professionally
printed books do not have the page
number at the start of each chapter,
so insert a section break at the end
of each chapter.

1. Check the Different First Page box
    in the header or footer menu.

2. At the end of each chapter,
    select Breaks and Next Page
    in the Page Layout tab.

3. Delete the header at the
    beginning of the chapter.

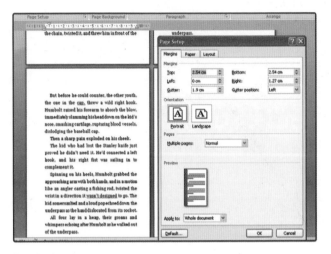

Step 3: Adjust the margins.

Hot Tip

If you need to adjust line spacing and text size
for your printed book, select all (Ctrl + A) and
right-click to bring up the Paragraph menu.

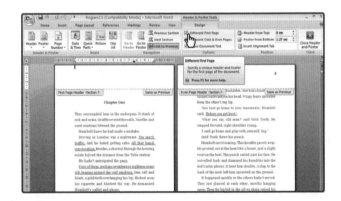

Step 1: Select the Different First Page box.

COVERS, BLURBS & METADATA

COVERS

The old saying suggests that you should never judge a book by its cover, yet your cover is the single most powerful tool for getting somebody interested in your work.

THE ROLE OF THE COVER

No matter how great a book is, the cover is what first grabs people's attention. A book with a poor cover is unlikely to sell many copies. Book covers are perhaps the most vital marketing tool for both e-books and printed books, but what makes a good cover can be subjective and it has to serve several functions.

- **Attention:** A cover should grab people's attention and make them want to take the book off the shelf (either actually or virtually).

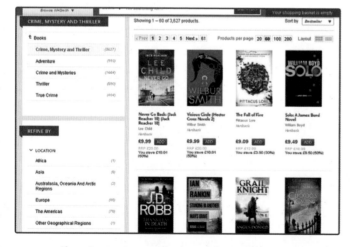

Above: An attractive cover will grab a reader's attention.

- **Tone:** A reader should be able to tell just by the cover what the genre is.

- **Brand:** Authors with an established brand can use similar elements on their covers to help readers to identify who they are.

- **Quality:** A book cover can be representative of the quality of a book.

E-BOOK COVERS

E-book covers do differ from those on printed books. The latter are designed for when books are displayed in physical bookstores. However, with an e-book, people view covers online.

Thumbnail

The first time a reader sees a book cover will be when it is in the listings on one of the vendor sites, such as Amazon. Usually, books are listed with just a thumbnail version of the cover, which is simply a shrunken image, enabling more books to appear in the listings. An e-book cover has to work on this small scale. Complicated covers with lots going on can be difficult to see when shrunk to thumbnails, which is why the best e-book covers tend to be simple.

Black and White

Some e-readers only operate in black and white, so you need to ensure that your book cover looks good in both full colour and greyscale.

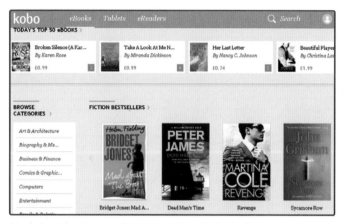

Above: Simple book covers work best when displayed as thumbnails.

Above: Search for books of a similar genre to get ideas for your own cover.

Hot Tip

When thinking about your cover, search for books in a similar genre and make a note of the similarities and common elements included.

WHAT MAKES A GOOD COVER?

Quantifying what makes a good book cover can be difficult. While some covers are artistically brilliant, they are not necessarily effective at grabbing a reader's attention. Likewise, a bold and simple design may not look artistic, but it could do the trick of standing out.

Colours

Since a good cover needs to stand out, bold, vibrant colours are often effective. However, colours need to work well together and not clash.

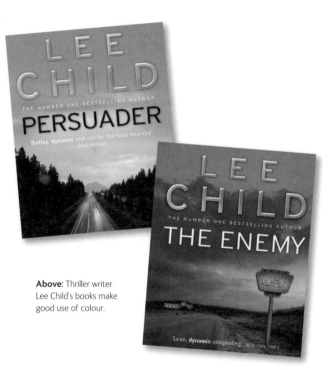

Above: Thriller writer Lee Child's books make good use of colour.

- **Number:** Avoid using more than three main colours.

- **Contrast:** If you use a bright, bold colour, match it with something subtle.

- **Avoid:** Primary colours, especially those default colours in image and design software. Go for shades instead.

- **Complementary:** Choose colours that complement each other, such as those that are opposite on the colour wheel, i.e. blues with oranges or purples with yellows.

- **Light and dark:** Use shadows and a combination of light and dark shades to create strong transitions that will attract the eye.

- **Experiment:** Test different colour combinations to see what works and what doesn't.

Elements

Elements are the different objects on a cover, such as the images and text. Some books

> ## Hot Tip
> **Use imagery that reflects your book. If you have written a thriller, think about including a gun or fast car on the cover if it fits with your story.**

are extremely busy, with lots of different elements, while others are simple and contain just an image, background, title and author name. Elements draw the eye, so they should not run into each other. Make sure there is ample space between them.

IMAGES

Most fiction authors place an image or two on the cover. Images can be photographs or artwork, which should be professionally produced (avoid home-made drawings unless you are a really talented artist). The purpose of cover images is not to describe the book, but to set the mood. For example, do

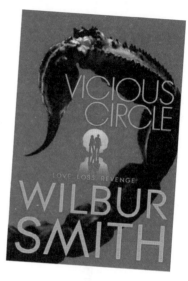

Below: *Vicious Circle* by Wilbur Smith stands out. It has only a few elements and three basic colours.

not try to represent your protagonists with a photograph. Readers will create their own mental image of your main characters when they read the book. Instead, put figures in silhouette or show a half-hidden profile.

Fonts

When searching for fonts, some people scour databases for obscure and unique ones. While this can ensure that you have fonts that other authors do not have, few readers will notice. The most important aspect of a font is that it should be easily readable. Make sure that it is as readable in thumbnail size as it is in full size, especially when it comes to the book's title.

- **Number:** Stick to two or three fonts maximum. Too many different ones will look messy.

- **Complementary:** Make sure that your fonts go together. A simple way to do this is to use one serif font (those with projections on them) and one sans serif font.

- **Simple:** Clever fonts, such as those that look like blood dripping off the page, may seem like a good idea, but can make the text difficult to read. Keep your fonts clean and simple.

- **Shadows and spacing:** Play around with the spacing on your letters and try effects such as shadows to make your fonts really stand out.

Above: Clive Cussler's books always have simple and easy-to-read fonts.

AUTHOR NAME, TITLE AND SUBTITLES

The most important words on the cover of any book are those in its title. While you may prefer your author name and any tagline to be small, your book's title has to stand out and be easy to read as a thumbnail. Subtitles and taglines can add an extra professional touch to a book cover, but are best placed at the top or bottom so that they do not get in the way of the other elements. In order to help develop a brand, ensure that your author name looks the same on all your books.

Above: Thriller writer Lisa Gardner's name appears the same way on all of her books.

CREATING A COVER

Whether you design your own cover or choose the services of a graphic designer, it has to look professional. If a cover looks amateurish or home-made, it will deter readers. Since a book cover has to sell your book, you should ensure that it is as functional as it is attractive. Think carefully about how you create yours. When it comes to producing a cover for an e-book, you have the following three options:

Hot Tip

Print out your cover in both full and thumbnail sizes before you publish your e-book. Get opinions from other people and make sure you ask if they can identify the book genre.

- ○ **Professional:** Hiring a third-party designer to create a bespoke cover for your book.

- ○ **Ready-made:** Plenty of places sell ready-made covers to which you can just add your title and author name.

- ○ **Do-it-yourself:** You can make your own covers using either graphics editing software or an online book creation service.

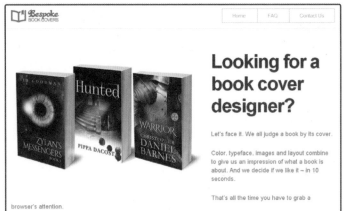

Above: Professional book cover designers such as bespokebookcovers.com are used by many self–published authors.

HIRING A COVER DESIGNER

By far the best solution for creating a cover for your book is to hire a professional to make one for you. However, bear in mind that not all graphic designers and artists can make a professional book cover. Cover creation is a specialist skill and you need to ensure that your cover designer has created book covers before and understands what makes a good one. The cost of a professional cover can vary, but expect to pay £300–£700 ($500–$1000) or even more to hire a highly experienced cover designer, especially if you want bespoke artwork.

Hot Tip

When hiring a cover designer, do a rough sketch of how you would like your book to look, scan it and send it to them.

Know What You Want

Before you hire a cover designer, you need to make sure that you know exactly what you want. Be certain that the designer knows what your book is about and what genre it belongs to, and discuss the sorts of elements you would like to see on your cover. Most designers allow for a number of revisions, but make sure that you know how many changes you can make.

BUYING A STOCK COVER

If you cannot afford to hire a designer to create a bespoke cover, you may wish to consider buying a ready-made cover. Book designers often create stock covers and can tailor these to suit your requirements. These often cost around £60–£120 ($100–$200). However, ensure that you choose something that fits your novel and that you have full copyright so that it will not appear on somebody else's book.

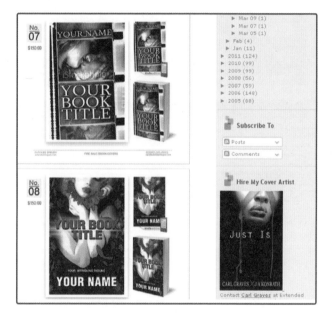

Above: Ready–made book covers for sale.

CREATING YOUR OWN COVER

For many new authors, the cost of professionally produced or ready-made covers is too much. After all, you don't know how much money your book will make, so it may be a long time before you recoup the several hundred pounds or dollars spent on a cover. For this reason, many self-published authors opt to create their own covers. However, cover creation requires some skill and experience in graphic design – or at least some artistic flair – so it really should be avoided unless you have no other choice or truly believe you can produce something good.

Online Services

One way to create your own cover is to use one of the many cover creation services you can find on the internet. These online services enable you to upload images and compile a cover using minimal knowledge and graphic design skills. Many of these online services make use of templates, which are easy to use but might result in your book cover looking similar to somebody else's.

Above: Amazon's KDP Cover Creator.

Above: Basic cover creator at www.readwritethink.org.

Cover Creation Services

Online cover creation services can vary in their complexity, but most are easy enough to use.

- **Amazon KDP**: Still in beta mode, Amazon's Cover Creator is really easy to use, but has the disadvantage of being the preferred online service for many KDP authors, so your cover may not look very original.

- **CreateSpace**: Have their own cover creator for making print book covers.

- **ReadWriteThink**: Free to use on their website (www.read writethink.org/files/resources/

interactives/bookcover/), this is an extremely basic cover creator aimed at students, but might suit somebody with limited graphic design experience.

- **www.ipiccy.com**: Primarily a free online photo editing suite, it can be used to create decent-looking covers.

- **www.myecovermaker.com**: Simple to use and with more templates than most online services, it enables you to come up with something unique.

Using Graphic Editing Software

Those with artistic flair or experience with computer-aided design (CAD) may wish to create their own cover from scratch using graphic editing programs such as Photoshop.

1. Run your editing program and create a blank template, ensuring it is a suitable e-book size (Amazon recommends a 1:6 aspect ratio, so you may want an image width of 1562 pixels and a height of 2500 pixels).

2. Create different layers for all your elements, such as background image, title and author name.

Step 1: Create a template in a suitable e-book size.

> ### Hot Tip
> If you are creating a POD book, CreateSpace will allow you to download your print cover for use with your e-book.

Resize [X]

New size: 89.5 MB

Resampling: Best Quality   *

○ By percentage: 100   %

◉ By absolute size:

☑ Maintain aspect ratio

Pixel size

Width: 1876   pixels
Height: 2500   pixels
Resolution: 96.00   pixels/inch

Print size

Width: 19.54   inches
Height: 26.04   inches

* Bicubic will be used

[OK]   [Cancel]

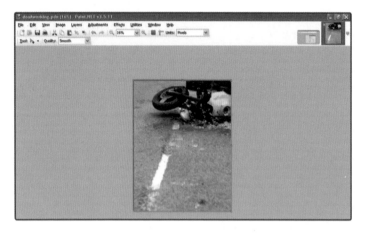

Step 3: Add a background image.

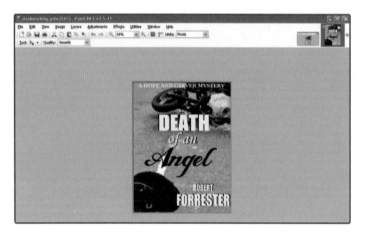

Step 4: Add other layer elements.

3. Add your background image first. Make changes to size and colours to suit your requirements.

4. Add other elements on a separate layer, then edit and position individually.

5. Save the image as a JPEG, ensuring you flatten it when prompted (making it one single layer).

Finding Images for Your Cover

When looking for images, you need to remember that you cannot use an image for your book cover unless you hold the copyright. This means that you cannot simply do an image search on the internet and take what you want.

Stock Images

One of the best resources for finding images is to use an image library. These contain thousands of stock images that can be downloaded and used. They are sold on a royalty-free basis, so you only have to pay once for each image and can use it as many times as you like. Expect to pay £5–£25 ($8–$40) for an image. The only downside of using stock images is that they are available to anyone, so you may find that your preferred picture is on the cover of another book.

Some of the most popular stock image libraries include the following:

- **iStockphoto**: One of the largest image libraries on the internet, with millions of images you can search through.

- **Shutterstock**: Another huge library of images which are available to peruse.

- **Dreamstime**: Here, you'll find a huge number of illustrations, as well as photographs you can use.

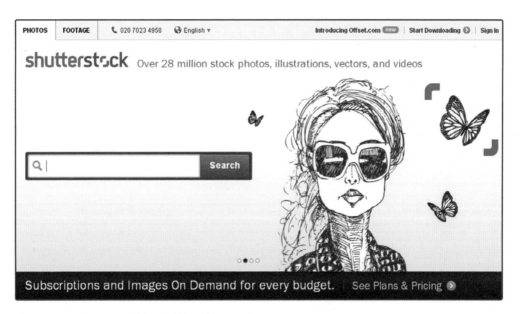

Above: Shutterstock is a source of downloadable stock images.

Hot Tip

If you are good behind the camera, try coming up with your own photographs. This will ensure that you have a cover image which is 100 per cent unique.

BLURBS

If you have created a good cover that has intrigued potential readers, the next step to encouraging them to download your e-book is to ensure that you have a good book description. However, condensing your novel into a few lines is not easy.

WHAT WAS LOST WILL BE FOUND

The Capitol Building, Washington DC: Harvard symbologist Robert Langdon believes he is here to give a lecture. He is wrong. Within minutes of his arrival, a shocking object is discovered. It is a gruesome invitation into an ancient world of hidden wisdom.

When Langdon's mentor, Peter Solomon – prominent mason and philanthropist – is kidnapped, Langdon realizes that his only hope of saving his friend's life is to accept this mysterious summons.

It is to take him on a breathless chase through Washington's dark history. All that was familiar is changed into a shadowy, mythical world in which Masonic secrets and never-before-seen revelations seem to be leading him to a single impossible and inconceivable truth...

'Unputdownable...Gripping...Jaw-dropping... The blockbuster read of the year' *NEWS OF THE WORLD*

'So compelling that several times I came close to a cardiac arrest...As perfectly constructed as the Washington architecture it escorts us around' *SUNDAY EXPRESS*

'A narrative that can grip you like a vice... As engaging a hero as you could wish for' *MAIL ON SUNDAY*

ISBN 978-0-552-14952-5

£7.99

FSC

Above: Descriptions on the backs of books should entice people to buy them.

BOOK DESCRIPTIONS

Book descriptions are often referred to as blurbs. With printed books, you normally find them on the back, but for e-books, they are on the product page on websites such as Amazon or Kobo. However, book descriptions can also be used for marketing, such as giving details about your book on social media or ensuring that readers know what it is about when they see it in search engine results.

Hot Tip

Read book descriptions from other novels in your genre. Try to identify common themes, ideas and styles.

PURPOSE OF A BLURB

A good blurb has to serve several purposes:

- **Describe**: It should explain the basic premise of your novel.

- **Sell**: A good blurb should sell your novel, as it is part of the sales process. A reader usually clicks on the thumbnail cover and then reads the blurb, before purchasing or reading a sample.

- **Tone**: A blurb should reflect the tone of your novel.

BLURB CONTENTS

Remember that a blurb is not a complete outline of your story. While some blurbs can encompass aspects of a synopsis, you should not give a step-by-step guide to what happens in the book; just outline what is at stake and for whom.

Character

All good blurbs have to introduce the main character of a story, as readers like to know who the protagonist is. This does not have to be a detailed description; you just need a few words to help readers identify what type of person they are dealing with, such as 'Tough inner-city cop John Smith', or 'Lonely sophomore Sarah Jones'.

After an epic and interrupted journey all the way from the snows of South Dakota, Jack Reacher has finally made it to Virginia. His destination: a sturdy stone building a short bus ride from Washington DC, the headquarters of his old unit, the 110th MP. It was the closest thing to a home he ever had.

Why? He wants to meet the new commanding officer, Major Susan Turner. He liked her voice on the phone. But the officer sitting behind Reacher's old desk isn't a woman. Why is Susan Turner not there?

What Reacher doesn't expect is what comes next. He himself is in big trouble, accused of a sixteen-year-old homicide. And he certainly doesn't expect to hear these words: *'You're back in the army, Major. And your ass is mine.'*

Will he be sorry he went back? Or – will someone else?

Above: The blurb on Lee Child's book *Never Go Back* describes the characters, conflict and themes of the book.

On a remote jungle island, genetic engineers have created a dinosaur game park.

An astonishing technique for recovering and cloning dinosaur DNA has been discovered. Now one of mankind's most thrilling fantasies has come true and the first dinosaurs that the Earth has seen in the time of man emerge.

But, as always, there is a dark side to the fantasy and after a catastrophe destroys the park's defence systems, the scientists and tourists are left fighting for survival...

'Crichton's most compulsive novel to date'
SUNDAY TELEGRAPH

Above: The blurb for Michael Crichton's *Jurassic Park* perfectly encapsulates the 'protagonist against nature' type of conflict.

Theme

A blurb should also describe any major themes in a book. If a novel is about love, betrayal or revenge, the blurb should help to bring this to the reader's attention. It should also be clear from reading the blurb to which genre the book belongs.

Conflict

At the very least, a blurb has to describe the basic conflict in your novel. In other words, it has to explain what is at stake. All novels have some sort of conflict: it is what drives the story and makes the characters do what they do. Conflicts create the tension, interest and excitement in a story, and most of them can be grouped into four different types:

- **Protagonist vs antagonist**: One character pitted against another. In a mystery, it could be the detectives trying to identify the criminal, or the romantic conflict between two characters in a romance.

- **Protagonist vs self**: Internal conflict where a character has to overcome his or her personal demons to triumph over adversity.

- **Protagonist vs society**: Common in thrillers, when a character has to battle against society (e.g. a person wrongly accused of a crime).

- **Protagonist vs nature**: Similar to protagonist vs antagonist, except that the protagonist is battling against a natural force rather than a human one.

WRITING A BLURB

Encapsulating all the main aspects of your story into a few well-chosen lines can be really challenging for an author. Many writers new to self-publishing make the mistake of trying to include too much information in their blurb. You need to strike a balance between capturing a reader's interest and providing enough intrigue so that they will want to read the book. Therefore, you should not give too much away.

Hot Tip

Keep paragraphs short, and use evocative and exciting words in your blurb, such as 'terrifying', 'betrayal' or 'revenge'.

Length

Blurbs should not be too long. When searching for books, readers do not want to read a 1,000-word description to understand what a book is about. With blurbs, the shorter the better. Aim for no more than 150 words, as it is better to keep readers wanting to know more than to bore them with an overly long book description.

Right: James Patterson's blurbs are always short.

Don't have a Kindle? Get your Kindle here, or download a **FREE** Kindle Reading App.

Trade-In Amazon.co.uk Gift Card? This offer is available the Books Trade-In Store for more details

Book Description

Release Date: **7 Nov 2013** | Series: **Alex Cross 21**

Alex Cross's whole world is crashing down around him.

He has been hunted, stalked like prey, his predator priming himself for the kill.

Cross has devoted his life to protecting others. Now he's unable to protect even those closest to him.

As a police detective, he has made many enemies, but never like this.

Everything he loves is being taken from him.

Soon he will have nothing and no one left.

Frequently Bought Together

Price For Both: £18.00

Add both to Basket

Show availability and delivery details

☑ **This item:** Cross My Heart (Alex Cross 21) by James Patterson Hardcover £9.00

CAPTURING READERS' ATTENTION

Your blurb has to attract readers to your book, hook them and make them want to know what happens. This can be really challenging. With such a short amount of space, every word in your blurb has to count, and it may take a lot of trial and error to edit down your blurb until it is right.

THE FLASHMAN PAPERS II
1842-43, 1847-48

WHEN A MISSION CALLS FOR A MASTER OF DISGUISE, DECEIT, LECHERY AND TREACHERY THERE'S ONLY ONE MAN FOR THE JOB –
FLASHMAN

Delivered by a legendary femme fatale into the clutches of the dastardly Otto von Bismarck, Flashman will need all his reserves of low cunning and seductive charm if he's to extricate himself from their fiendish plot. From London's gaming-halls to the dungeons and throne-rooms of Europe, our hero engages in a desperate succession of escapes, amours and a bit of unavoidable swordplay while the destiny of a continent rests on his quivering shoulders.

"Fraser writes delightfully; his sense of period and dialogue is perfect; his hero is irresistible. Many popular novelists have written fictional heroes into great historical

Above: This book has a present tense, comedic blurb to match the tone of the novel.

Tense

Most blurbs are written in the present tense. In other words, rather than writing that something 'was' happening, write that something 'is' happening. This provides a sense of immediacy and makes it seem like the events in the novel are taking place now, thus encouraging a reader to find out what happens.

Voice

You need to write a blurb in the same voice as your novel and, therefore, if you have written a comedy, you should inject humour into it. Your blurb has to reflect your writing style too. Think of it as an advertisement for your work. Of course, your blurb should also be free from any errors in spelling, grammar and punctuation.

YOUR OPENING

Just as any novel needs a great opening sentence to hook a reader, so does a blurb. Your first line has to attract a reader and persuade them to read more. In addition, the first 155 characters are usually what search engines display when people are doing book searches, so the opening has to be strong. Several techniques can help you to grab a reader's attention:

- ○ **Tagline**: Summarize the conflict, themes and outline in a single sentence.

- ○ **Pose a question**: Ask readers what they would do if they faced the same conflict as played out in your novel.

- ○ **Mystery**: Create intrigue to spark a reader's curiosity.

- ○ **Character**: Introduce your character straightaway and try to make readers care about what happens to them.

Copyrighted Material

AN UNFLINCHING PORTRAIT OF A FAMILY TORN APART BY VIOLENCE AND BETRAYAL, BUT ULTIMATELY BOUND BY LOYALTY, BY BLOOD, AND BY A BURNING DESIRE FOR REVENGE...

The Bailey brothers are gangsters determined to make their mark on the world. Peter and Daniel are chalk and cheese in many ways, but together they are unstoppable. From the late seventies they rule London's East End and it seems that no one can touch them. It's never easy at the top though, and there is always someone waiting to take you down – sometimes even those closest to you...

Daniel's wife Lena is determined to shield their daughter Tania from the Life. But when a terrible tragedy occurs, Tania's eyes

Above: Taglines are often used to describe the conflict and themes in books.

THE ENDING

Just as important as the beginning of your blurb is the end, as you want to leave readers wanting to know more. If possible, end on a cliffhanger, or make readers believe that the outcome is uncertain.

Hot Tip

Use capitals, bold words, italics and ellipses in your blurbs to draw your readers' eyes to certain words or situations.

KEYWORDS

Since readers discover books by using the search engines in online bookstores, you need to include keywords in your blurb to help with discoverability. Try to include one or two keyword phrases, especially in the first 50 words, but make sure that the blurb still reads naturally and the keywords do not sound forced (for more information on keywords, see the section on metadata, pages 140–49).

REFINING YOUR BLURB

Rewrite and edit your blurb until you are 100 per cent happy with it. Do several versions and ask a few people for their opinion as to which is the best. Do not be afraid to make changes to your blurb; if your book is not selling, redo the blurb and see if that makes a difference, as sometimes a new blurb can dramatically improve sales. However, make sure that you keep the older version, as you may want to change it back.

WRITING BLURBS FOR DIFFERENT MEDIA

The product page of online retailers is not the only place where you can use your blurb to attract the attention of readers. Blurbs are a great tool to use on social media and other platforms to advertise your book. However, this means that you will need different blurbs to fit each medium.

Online Retailers

Different online retailers have different limits and requirements for book descriptions. Some ask for a full-length description, as well as a briefer version. This means writing a short (350 characters) blurb description to go with a longer version, which can be extremely tricky, because then you have to condense your blurb even more.

Social Media

Twitter and other social media platforms can be a great way to advertise your book, and the best way to do this is to send your blurb to people. However, with only 140 characters to play with, and the need for enough space to post a link and possibly a hashtag, you will need to condense your blurb to fewew than 100 characters.

Above: A book blurb condensed for a tweet.

METADATA

In order for people to discover your books, you need to ensure that you have attached all the relevant information about it. Metadata is an essential part of self-publishing, but not everybody gets it right.

WHAT IS METADATA?

Metadata sounds like quite a technical term, and it is something that is mentioned a lot in internet magazines and blogs. However, metadata is just information. The internet and online e-book retailers run on data, so without metadata, nobody could discover your book. In the e-book world, metadata includes everything that helps people to discover, sell and categorize your book. For e-books, metadata falls into the following two categories:

- **Core:** Essential information that all books need in order to help people find and categorize them, such as the price, category, title and author name.

Editorial Reviews

About the Author
Robert Forrester is a writer and journalist based in Birmingham, United Kingdom. Among other things, he is th[e]
Inspector Anderson Mysteries, Hope and Carver Mysteries, the thriller Rogues, and various short fiction that he
anthologies and literary magazines.

Product Details
File Size: 431 KB
Print Length: 174 pages
Simultaneous Device Usage: Unlimited
Publisher: Best of Both Worlds (August 4, 2013)
Sold by: Amazon Digital Services, Inc.
Language: English
ASIN: B00CR1E5ME
Text-to-Speech: Enabled ☑
X-Ray: Not Enabled ☑
Lending: Not Enabled
Amazon Best Sellers Rank: #49,799 Paid in Kindle Store (See Top 100 Paid in Kindle Store)
   #82 in Kindle Store > Kindle eBooks > Mystery, Thriller & Suspense > Suspense > Paranormal

Did we miss any relevant features for this product? Tell us what we missed.
Would you like to give feedback on images or tell us about a lower price?

Customer Reviews

Above: Book metadata as displayed on the product information page on Amazon.

Hot Tip

Most online retailers allow you to assign two major categories to your book. Make sure that you take advantage of both for maximum discoverability and include the two most relevant categories applicable to your story.

○ **Enhanced**: Additional information that is nonessential, but which can help people learn more about a book, such as product reviews, an author biography and sample chapters.

BOOK CATEGORIES

Perhaps the primary use of metadata is in helping readers find books that they want to read. For this, all e-books require categories.

BISAC and BIC

Traditionally, bookstores have used formal categorizing systems known as BISAC in North America (Book Industry Standards and Communications) and BIC (Book Industry Communication) in some European countries (including the UK) and Australia. These standards are governed by the Book Industry Study Group (BISG) in the USA and BIC in the UK, and ensure that all bookshops and libraries place

Above: The Book Industry Study Group governs the categorizing systems in the US.

the same books in the same categories and know how to order books of a certain genre. Both BISAC and BIC categories work in a similar way, i.e. they assign a code that describes the type of book, followed by its genre and subgenre written out.

For example:

FIC022080	FICTION/Mystery & Detective/International Mystery & Crime
FIC028020	FICTION/Science Fiction/Hard Science Fiction

ONLINE CATEGORIES

Some online retailers base their category systems on the BISAC and BIC systems, although Amazon has developed its own category system, which uses its own data. Amazon introduces new subcategories to its system quite frequently, enabling readers to narrow down their search for books. However, many of these subcategories are based on other metadata, such as keywords and blurb information, and even other titles that readers of the book have purchased. This means that authors and publishers cannot necessarily choose to categorize their books into certain subgenres, but may find that they appear in those based on the book's metadata.

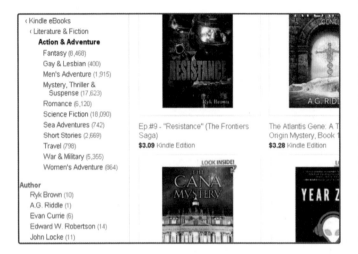

Above: Amazon has developed its own category system, which it constantly updates.

Left: Assigning a category on Amazon KDP.

> ## Hot Tip
>
> **Amazon also has bestseller lists in all its categories and subcategories, which means that in some of the more obscure subcategories, you may find you are on the bestseller list, even if you have only sold a handful of copies.**

INDIVIDUAL BOOK INFORMATION

All books have metadata that is unique to them. Some of this is obvious, such as the title or author name, but other information is also important.

Above: An ISBN is necessary for all books and e-books that are published.

ISBN

All books are assigned individual identification numbers, and traditionally, all of them were part of the International Standard Book Number (ISBN) system. This number describes both the publisher and book title. Authors and publishers have to buy an ISBN for each book or e-book published. However, services such as Smashwords and CreateSpace often assign self-published authors a free ISBN, but this does mean that these platforms become the official publisher of the title. You can, of course, purchase your own ISBNs, and you can do this through self-publishing platforms or from companies such as www.isbnservices.com.

ASIN

Unlike most other e-book platforms, Amazon does not require an ISBN. Instead, all books and e-books on the website are assigned an Amazon Standard Identification Number (ASIN). Amazon automatically assigns an ASIN for all e-books published in its KDP program. For traditionally published titles, the ASIN is normally the same as the ISBN. Some other online retailers, such as Barnes & Noble, now assign their own unique ID numbers too.

Price

The price of a book title is also a crucial piece of metadata. In today's global marketplace, all books should have a US, UK and Euro price as a minimum. Most e-book platforms are US-based, so prices are originally set in US dollars and converted for various territories. However, Amazon lets you assign an individual price for each country. This allows you to make prices more typical of what you might expect (£2.99 instead of £2.73, for example).

Note that in Europe e-books are subject to sales tax (VAT), so make sure that you calculate the effect of an added three per cent on your price.

			35% (Why?)	n/a	$1.05
Amazon.com	$ 2.99 USD Price must be between $2.99 and $9.99.		70%	$0.04	$2.06
Amazon.in (What's this?)	☑ Set IN price automatically based on US price ₪170		70%	₪2	₪118
Amazon.co.uk	☐ Set UK price automatically based on US price £ 1.92 GBP Price must be between £1.49 and £7.81.		70%	£0.03	£1.32
Amazon.de	☑ Set DE price automatically based on US price €2.60		70%	€0.03	€1.80
Amazon.fr	☑ Set FR price automatically based on US price €2.60		70%	€0.03	€1.80

Above: Amazon allows you to set different prices for different countries.

> ## Hot Tip
>
> Take advantage of the .99 ending to a price. This is a powerful psychological tool. A reader may baulk at paying $5 for an e-book, but may be perfectly happy to pay $4.99.

DISCOVERABILITY

While categories can help readers to discover books, they are not the only way for people to find books on retail sites, as most of them use search engines.

Search Engines

Search engines are a critical aspect of the online world. Most people will have used websites such as Google and Yahoo to find products and services on the internet. However, when it comes to selling books, the search engines used by e-book retailers are far more important. The most famous is Amazon's 'Recommendation Engine', which uses powerful algorithms based on metadata, as well as people's individual buying habits, to list books in which they may be interested. These search engines are what many readers use to discover books, and therefore ensuring that your titles contain the right metadata to aid discoverability is crucial.

> Tags
> Enter one or more keywords with which to tag your book. Enter each tag, one at a time, into the field below and click the "Add Tag" button to add it. (You may also remove tags by clicking the "Remove" link that appears next to them.)
>
> As you type each keyword, suggestions for common tags used by other Smashwords authors may pop up below the field. You may click one to add it to your book's tags. Tagging this way creates 'folksonomy' that will make it easier for readers to find books about subjects they're interested in. (Tags may contain letters, numbers and spaces.)
>
> **thriller** (Remove), **mercenaries** (Remove), **war** (Remove), **action adventure** (Remove), **mens adventure** (Remove), **special forces** (Remove), **military fiction** (Remove), **creature horror** (Remove), **africa adventure** (Remove)
>
> `suspense`   [Add Tag]
>
> suspense
> suspense action
> suspense action
> adventure climbing
> flying peru floatplane
> carribbean travel
> suspense action book
> suspense action
> ebook
> suspense action
> empowerment women
> suspense action in the

Above: Assign relevant keywords to help people find your book.

KEYWORDS

You can assign keywords to your e-books in order to help readers using search engines on retail sites to find them. Different online retailers let you provide varying numbers of keywords to your books. Amazon allows a maximum of seven, and you really need to take advantage of all of them to maximize discoverability and to give you the best chance of being found when readers do searches.

Using Keywords

Keywords can be a single term or multiple words. They can describe the type of book, the setting, character type (such as detective or soldier), a subgenre or any words that people may use to look for titles. You should separate keywords with a comma, and it is a good idea to refrain from using the same words used by your categories, as these will already be assigned to your title. The best way to use keywords effectively is to do your research and think about all the terms that readers may use in search boxes.

- ○ **Make a list**: Write down a list of all the words that describe your book and what it is about.

- ○ **Search**: Do searches using these words and see which other titles come up.

- ○ **Results**: Use the keywords that generate the most results.

Hot Tip
If you are creating your own e-book files using programs such as Calibre, you can add tags using the metadata function.

Above: Amazon KDP allows you to assign up to seven keywords.

ADVANCED METADATA

Where you appear on search pages is based on keywords and your book's relevance to a search query, but other types of metadata also have an effect.

Bestselling Ranks

One thing that can affect how high up a book appears in a search result is its bestselling rank, i.e. the popularity of a book. Not all online retailers use sales ranks in their search algorithms, but Amazon does. Sales ranks also appear on the product description page, which can help to influence a purchasing decision, because readers often like to buy books that are popular with other people.

In addition to the bestselling rank, Amazon also shows if a book is in the top 100 of a category bestseller list, which can also influence purchasing decisions.

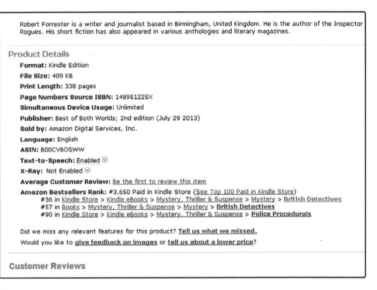

Robert Forrester is a writer and journalist based in Birmingham, United Kingdom. He is the author of the Inspector Rogues. His short fiction has also appeared in various anthologies and literary magazines.

Product Details

Format: Kindle Edition
File Size: 409 KB
Print Length: 338 pages
Page Numbers Source ISBN: 148951225X
Simultaneous Device Usage: Unlimited
Publisher: Best of Both Worlds; 2nd edition (July 29 2013)
Sold by: Amazon Digital Services, Inc.
Language: English
ASIN: B00CVBOSWW
Text-to-Speech: Enabled ☑
X-Ray: Not Enabled ☑
Average Customer Review: Be the first to review this item
Amazon Bestsellers Rank: #3,650 Paid in Kindle Store (See Top 100 Paid in Kindle Store)
    #36 in Kindle Store > Kindle eBooks > Mystery, Thriller & Suspense > Mystery > British Detectives
    #57 in Books > Mystery, Thriller & Suspense > Mystery > **British Detectives**
    #90 in Kindle Store > Kindle eBooks > Mystery, Thriller & Suspense > **Police Procedurals**

Did we miss any relevant features for this product? **Tell us what we missed.**
Would you like to **give feedback on images** or **tell us about a lower price**?

Customer Reviews

Above: The sales and bestselling ranks as displayed on Amazon.

Recommendation Lists

Amazon has a recommendation facility, which lists some of the other titles that people have purchased before they bought your book. If you appear on another book's 'Also bought' list, it can dramatically improve your own discoverability, depending on the popularity of the book in question.

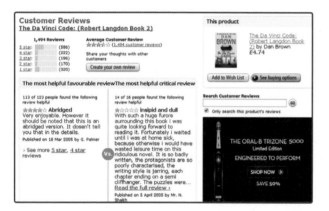

Above: Including editorial reviews is an excellent way to encourage readers to buy your book.

Above: Customer reviews can have a powerful influence on potential readers.

Hot Tip

Some authors have taken to buying reviews or posting their own under fake accounts, but this is dishonest and online retailers now have a zero-tolerance approach to such activities.

REVIEWS, AWARDS AND BIOGRAPHY

While there is little you can do to aid your book's appearance in the 'Also bought', rankings and bestseller lists, you can use other metadata to help convince readers to purchase your book. If your title has received positive reviews in magazines or blogs, or has won an award, you can include this information on the product page for your book. This could convince readers that what you are offering is a worthwhile purchase. In addition, readers like to know a little about the author, so including a brief biography can also help when it comes to convincing people to purchase a title.

CUSTOMER REVIEWS

Most online websites have a review system where customers can review and assign a star rating to a book. As books with the largest number of high ratings tend to sell more copies than books with fewer and lower ratings, the review system has become a powerful sales tool.

SERIES TITLE

If a book is part of a series, most online retailers allow you to include the series information on the product page. This can help readers to find further books in the series, which can improve your sales, because if a reader liked the first book, there is a good chance that they may wish to read the next one.

BOOK SAMPLE

Another powerful sales tool is the sample. Most online retailers permit readers to look at a sample of the book before purchasing it. This is normally the first chapter or two, but is usually based on a percentage of the entire work, such as five or 10 per cent. Therefore, you really do need to ensure that the beginning of your book reads brilliantly. Always check what the sample looks like when you publish your book, to make sure that the formatting is perfect, and structure the beginning of your e-book so that readers don't have to flick through pages and pages of superfluous information before the actual story starts.

Above: Most online retailers, like Amazon, allow you to enter a series title.

Chapter One

They surrounded him in the underpass. It stank of sick and urine. Graffiti covered the walls. Needles and used condoms littered the ground.

Humbolt knew he had made a mistake.

Driving in London was a nightmare. Too much traffic. And he hated getting cabs. All that banal conversation. Besides, a shortcut through the housing estate halved the distance from the Tube station.

He hadn't anticipated the gang.

Four of them, perhaps seventeen or eighteen-years-old, leaning against the wall smoking. One, tall and black, a gold tooth overhanging his lip, flicked away his cigarette and blocked the way. He demanded Humbolt's wallet and phone.

'You're in our yard, old man,' the youth said, spitting sideways through his teeth. 'You have to pay the toll.'

The others encircled. The biggest, a white kid in a heavy jacket, had a silver chain around his neck. The other two

Above: Make sure that your book sample reads enticingly and that it looks good.

DISTRIBUTING YOUR DIGITAL PRODUCT

PRICE

Without the high production costs associated with printed books, e-books can be priced much lower, but how low is too low? And is there an optimum price for your work?

E-BOOK PRICING

E-book pricing is a highly complicated and much discussed topic. Unlike printed books, which have set costs attached, such as printing and distribution, the production costs of e-books are much lower and, therefore, consumers expect the price to reflect this. In addition, an e-book is not a physical product, but virtual, so readers are reluctant to pay the same sort of price as they would for something that they can own and place on their shelves.

Above: E-book prices can vary greatly.

Range

If you look at the websites of e-book retailers, you will see that prices vary dramatically. For some traditionally published books, the e-book is often not much cheaper than the hardback or paperback, while some indie authors are selling their books for just a few pence or cents. This disparity means that pricing your novel requires a lot of thought, taking into account many variables.

Low and High

There are two schools of thought when it comes to setting the price of an e-book, especially for new authors.

- **Cheap**: If you set your price as low as possible, you are likely to sell more copies and attract readers who may not want to chance more money on a new author.

- **High value**: Production costs may be lower, but the price of an e-book should reflect the time and effort spent writing it, and cheap e-books risk devaluing authors.

PRICING STRATEGY

No one price is suitable for all authors. You really need to think about your goals. If reaching the largest reader base is more important than making money, price your book low, but if you want to earn enough to reflect all your hard work and provide a useful income, you will need to come up with a pricing strategy.

Hot Tip

In your pricing strategy, remember to factor in the costs associated with creating your e-book, such as editing, cover design and formatting.

Sales vs Readership

When bestselling author John Locke sold over a million e-books, they were all priced at $0.99. If he had priced his books any higher, he may not have sold anywhere near as many, but may have made the same amount of money. However, reaching fewer readers could have meant that John Locke would have sold fewer copies of subsequent books; therefore, pricing low is a way to build up an author platform and, in the long term, could make you more money, but it is not without its problems.

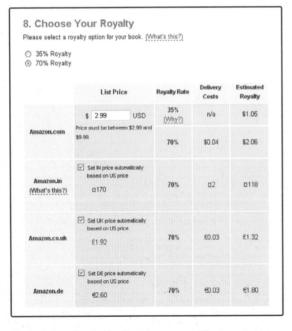

Above: Amazon allows you to choose between two different royalty rates.

ROYALTY RATES

The following dollar-to-pound conversions are based on the rate when this book was written, but will vary depending on the current exchange rate. In addition, some conversions are based on Amazon's minimum threshold rates and include VAT, which is added to e-books for sale in the UK and

Europe. At the time of writing, this was currently set at the Luxembourg rate of three per cent, but may be subject to change.

Many e-book retailers have a fixed royalty rate for e-book sales. However, Amazon, by far the largest market, has a two-tier rate, which is aimed at encouraging authors to price their books within a range that the company considers the most appropriate for e-books.

- ◯ **70 per cent**: Amazon pays 70 per cent royalties on all e-books priced between $2.99 and $9.99 (£1.49 and £7.81)

- ◯ **35 per cent**: Amazon pays 35 per cent royalties for all e-books priced below $2.99 and higher than $9.99.

Calculating Royalties

The minimum price for selling an e-book through Amazon's KDP platform is $0.99. However, because of their two-tier royalty rate, you need to sell nearly six times more books priced at this rate (with each one paying you $0.35 in royalties) to make the same amount of money as selling one book priced at $2.99 (each sale making you $2.00).

Above: E–book prices often correspond to the length of the book. For example, this short story has been priced at just £0.77.

VALUING YOUR WORK

Some authors prefer to price their books to reflect the effort that went into them or the value they offer a reader. This can mean pricing a book based on how long it is. For instance, if you have a 300-page novel priced at £2.70 ($3.99), you may want to price a 150-page novella at £1.79 ($2.99) and a 30-page short story at £0.77 ($0.99).

Perception

Although giving your e-book a low price can lead to more sales, it can also have the opposite effect. Some readers will not buy books if they are priced too low, as they may perceive the quality to be poor. Some readers also do not like the idea of self-published books and often look at low price points as an indicator that a book has not been professionally published. Yet they may buy the same book if priced higher, simply because they think that the quality will be better.

Competition

Another factor to consider when coming up with a pricing strategy is the cost of other books in your genre. You do not want your book to be higher in price than similar titles, as readers will possibly choose the cheaper books over yours. However, you do not want your price to appear too low, as readers may perceive your work to be 'cheap' compared to others. Make sure that you look at what other authors are charging and find a happy medium.

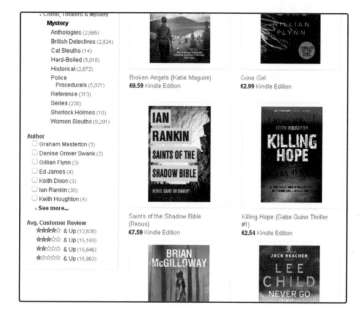

Above: Compare the prices of books in the same genre. to assess how to price your own book.

PRICE TRENDS

As there are many aspects to pricing an e-book, it can often be helpful to analyse statistical trends. Fortunately, one of the big e-book platforms has done some research on pricing, which has generated some interesting results.

Smashwords' Study

E-book aggregator and retailer Smashwords examined its data on e-book sales relating to their prices each year, and it revealed certain trends.

- **Low price points:** The $0.99–$1.99 (£0.77–£1.50) range remains very popular with self-published e-books, but they do not perform as well as other price points.

- **Most common:** $2.99 (£2.00) is the most popular price for self-published books.

- **Most effective:** E-books priced at $3.99 perform just as well as books priced at $2.99.

- **High price points:** Books priced up to $6.99 (£4.70) continue to sell well, but sales of books priced higher than this are not as good.

EXPERIMENTATION

One of the great advantages that self-published authors have over those published traditionally is the ability to experiment with prices. Not having any of the large overheads associated with publishing houses, indie authors are able to undercut traditionally published e-books as well as change prices at will to boost sales, income or both.

- **Start low:** If you price an e-book at a low price point, you can gradually raise the price to see what effect it has on sales.

Above: Discounting prices for a limited time may encourage people to buy your books.

- **Start high:** Release an e-book at a higher price point, and lower the price to see if it increases sales.

- **Maximize profits:** You can adjust your price to find the sweet spot that maximizes profits in relation to sales numbers.

Pricing Promotions

This freedom to change prices enables indie authors to run price promotions and also to put different books at different prices; for example, you could place the first book in a series at a lower price in order to generate more readers who may go on to buy subsequent titles.

ONLINE SELLING

Once you have written, edited and formatted your e-book, created a cover, and decided on a price, it is time to sell your novel to readers. The internet enables you to reach millions of potential readers, and in this section, we will explore all the available options for online selling.

ONLINE RETAIL

In many ways, selling e-books online is no different to selling other products over the internet. You can sell directly on your own website or through online vendors, such as Amazon, Apple and Kobo. However, the great advantage of selling e-books is that they are not physical products, so you do not have to worry about delivery and shipping costs. When you sell an e-book, you simply upload your title and your customers can download it directly to their computer or e-reader.

Selling Online

In order to sell an e-book through the numerous vendors and online retailers, you have two options:

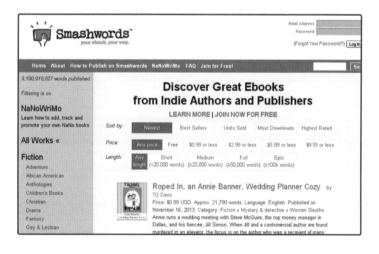

- **Direct:** Uploading straight to vendor platforms.

- **Aggregator:** Going through an aggregator service that will distribute your e-book to the major online vendors.

Above: E-book aggregators, such as Smashwords, distribute books to online vendors for you.

REACH

Having your e-book listed on as many websites and online bookstores as you can is the best way to ensure that you are reaching the widest possible audience. If you only sell one copy on each retailer each month, this can result in dozens of sales in total. However, different retailers have different numbers of customers and therefore, in order to maximize your reach, you need to ensure that you are selling on the most popular e-book platforms.

Above: Amazon is the world's number one online e-book retailer.

- **Amazon**: The world's number one online e-book retailer, it receives millions of customers each week.

- **Kobo**: Dominant in Canada and Australia, where it even outsells Amazon, Kobo is also popular in the UK, especially as it distributes to WH Smith.

- **Barnes & Noble**: The USA's most popular high street bookstore, it also has its own e-reader: the Nook.

- **Apple**: The iBook Store is very popular with Apple device users.

- **Sony**: Although not as popular as the Kindle or Nook, the Sony Reader still has a solid following.

Hot Tip

Many self-published authors find that Amazon sales exceed the combined sales from all the other retailers.

AGGREGATORS

If you do an online search for e-books, you will find hundreds of different websites selling them, which may leave you wondering how you can possibly upload your novel to every store. The answer is to use one of the many aggregator services, which will distribute your title for you. Some of these platforms are free, while others charge a set fee.

- **Smashwords**: The most popular e-book aggregator for self-published authors. By publishing on Smashwords, you can reach the Apple iBook Store, Barnes & Noble, Sony Reader Store, Kobo, Baker & Taylor and many more.

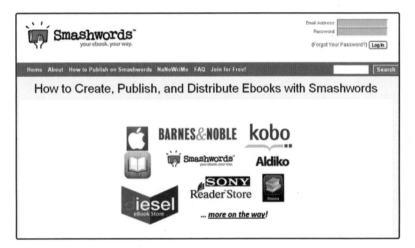

Above: Smashwords distributes to all of these major vendors.

- **Lulu**: Offers free distribution to the Apple iBook Store, Barnes & Noble and the Lulu Marketplace.

- **Booktango**: A free service that will distribute to Barnes & Noble, Apple iBook Store, Kobo, Sony, Google and Scribd.

- **BookBaby**: Their basic package ($99/£65) includes distribution to Apple's iBook Store, Amazon, Barnes & Noble, Sony Reader Store and Kobo.

Hot Tip

Many aggregator services offer only limited distribution to Amazon, so if you wish to ensure that your books are listed on Amazon.com, you need to use the KDP platform.

Advantages of E-book Aggregators

Going through an e-book aggregator has plenty of advantages for the self-published author.

- ○ **Time**: You only have to upload your e-book once and the aggregator will send it to all the main retailers and platforms for you.

- ○ **Conversion**: Instead of having to create different e-book file formats for the various retailers, most aggregator services will convert your file for you.

> ## Hot Tip
> Smashwords pays authors a royalty of 60 per cent for sales through retailers and 85 per cent for sales through their own website.

- ○ **Reach**: Some online retailers do not have the facilities for you to self-publish directly, so the only way to reach them is through an aggregator.

iBooks
A novel way to buy and read books.
Be well read with iBooks and all its latest features. Download the iBooks app from the App Store. Then fill your iPhone, iPod touch or iPad library with books from the iBook Store. Take them to more places than you'd ever take a normal book. And from the moment you pull one out, you'll be pulled in.

Above: The iBook Store requires an Apple device in order to submit your e-book directly to it.

- ○ **Territory**: You cannot upload to some retailers if you are in a different country, so an aggregator may be your only option to have your title listed on these websites.

- ○ **Apple**: If you do not have an Apple device, using an aggregator is the only way to get your e-book to the Apple Store.

- ○ **Tracking**: It is much easier to keep track of sales and royalties if they are all in one place.

Disadvantages of E-book Aggregators

While there are many advantages to aggregator services, they do come with their downsides.

○ **Cost**: You either have to pay a set fee to use an aggregator service or they will take a commission on each sale.

○ **Delay**: It can take weeks to get your book listed on some of the partner sites, whereas going directly to them can take just days or even hours. In addition, it can take several months before royalties reach you from the various retailers.

○ **Control**: Going through a third party can be awkward. For instance, it can take several weeks for any amendments you make on an e-book to reach the various different retailers.

Channel	Retailer Sales Reported Through	Your Smashwords Balance Adjusted For Retailer Sales Through
Smashwords.com	Today	Today
Sony	Nov 9, 2013	Sep 30, 2013
Barnes & Noble	Nov 7, 2013 For non-free titles. Oct 1, 2013 For free titles.	Aug 31, 2013
Kobo	Sep 30, 2013 For non-free titles. Aug 31, 2011 For free titles.	Sep 30, 2013
Amazon	Sep 30, 2013	Aug 31, 2013
Apple	Nov 2, 2013 For non-free titles. Oct 31, 2013 For free titles.	Aug 31, 2013
Diesel	Oct 31, 2013	Aug 31, 2013
Page Foundry	Sep 30, 2013	Aug 31, 2013
Baker & Taylor Blio	Sep 30, 2013	Jul 31, 2013
Library Direct	Jun 21, 2013	Jun 21, 2013

Above: The Smashwords royalty channel can take three months to update from some retailers.

Calculating Costs

While some services, such as Smashwords and Lulu, offer free distribution, if you go on to sell large numbers of books, you may be better off paying the one-off fee for a paid-for service rather than using a free service that charges a commission on each sale.

UPLOADING TO SMASHWORDS

For many self-published authors, Smashwords is the simplest method of getting their work distributed to all the major retailers. Over 250,000 e-books have been uploaded through Smashwords since 2009. However, getting through their uploading platform, the Meatgrinder, does cause problems for some authors.

Step 3: Enter the title and description for your book.

Step 6: Choose the various formats.

1. Sign up to Smashwords by visiting www.smashwords.com/signup.

2. Click Publish on the homepage once you have logged in.

3. Fill in the title and description (blurb) for your books.

4. Select a price for your e-book in dollars and choose how much of your novel you want readers to see in the sample.

5. Choose your book's category and select keyword tags that best describe it.

6. Choose which formats you want your book to be converted into.

7. Upload your cover image and e-book file, either as a .doc file or ePub format.

8. Click Publish to begin the upload and conversion process.

Auto-vetting

After you have clicked Publish, your e-book file will be uploaded to Smashwords and converted to the different e-book formats for the various vendors. However, before Smashwords will distribute your book, it has to go through the auto-vetter process. This automatically checks the files for common errors. If the auto-vetter detects an issue, Smashwords will email you with the problem and provide guidance on a solution.

ISBN

Once your e-book has gone through the auto-vetting system, it will be available for sale on the Smashwords website. However, before Smashwords will distribute your book to the various vendors, you have to attach an ISBN to your e-book. Smashwords provides these free (see pages 143–44).

1. Click Dashboard on the Smashwords homepage.

2. On the right-hand side, click where it says ISBN Manager.

3. Select the title you are publishing and click Assign ISBN.

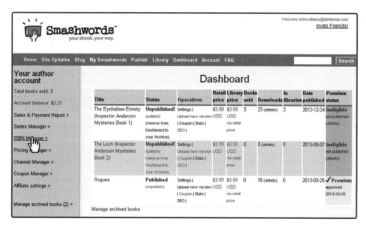

Step 2: Click on the ISBN manager.

Premium Catalog

Once you have assigned an ISBN to your book, you can apply to have it listed in Smashwords' Premium Catalog. This simply means that the title will be distributed to all their e-book retailers. However, since each vendor has specific requirements, every e-book has to be vetted manually, which can take several weeks. After this process, you will receive an email telling you whether your e-book is listed in the Premium Catalog, or if the vetter has discovered any errors or issues that need correction.

Hot Tip

Smashwords produces a style guide to assist self-published authors in getting through their auto-vetting procedure. This is available to download as a free e-book on their website.

The Dashboard

In order to see the status of your e-book, click Dashboard, where you will find various tools that can help you to manage your e-books.

○ **Channel Manager:** Choose to which vendors you want your e-book to be sent.

○ **Sales & Payment Report:** See your royalties and current sales.

○ **Pricing Manager:** Adjust the cover price for your e-books.

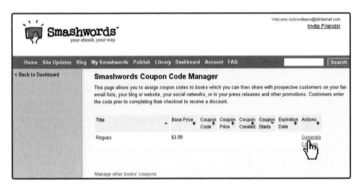

Above: Smashwords allows you to generate a discount coupon.

○ **Settings:** Make changes to your metadata, or upload a new version of your e-book or cover.

○ **Coupon Manager:** Lets you generate coupons so that your friends and family can download your book for free or at a discount.

Hot Tip

Due to its market dominance, many self-published authors opt to upload directly to Amazon and then use an aggregator for all the other retailers.

UPLOADING DIRECTLY TO RETAILERS

Uploading directly to retailer sites has its advantages. Firstly, you don't have to pay a third party any of your royalties, and secondly, you can get your book distributed much more quickly. Of course, it is not feasible or possible to upload your e-book to every retailer on the internet, but you can upload directly to the most popular online stores, such as Amazon or Kobo.

KINDLE DIRECT PUBLISHING

If you are self-publishing a novel and you want to reach the widest possible audience, you really need to take advantage of Kindle Direct Publishing (KDP). In order to sign up to KDP, just visit https://kdp.amazon .com/self-publishing/signin, or click the 'Independently Publish with Us' link at the bottom of Amazon's homepage and then fill in your details.

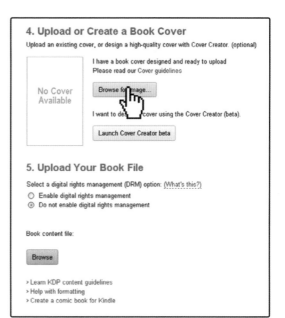

Step 1: Click the 'Add new title' button on the KDP dashboard.

Uploading Your E-book to KDP

1. After you sign up/log in, you will be taken to the KDP dashboard. In order to upload an e-book, simply click the yellow 'Add new title' button.

2. Choose whether to enrol the book in the KDP Select program (*see* page 196).

3. Enter the name, publisher (if applicable) and other metadata for your book, including description, categories and keywords.

4. Upload your cover image or use the cover creator to create one and then upload your e-book file (KDP accepts .doc, PDF or Mobi files).

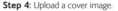

Step 4: Upload a cover image.

		35% (Why?)	n/a	$1.05
Amazon.com	$ 2.99 USD Price must be between $2.99 and $9.99.	70%	$0.04	$2.06
Amazon.in (What's this?)	☑ Set IN price automatically based on US price □170	70%	□2	□118
Amazon.co.uk	☐ Set UK price automatically based on US price £ 1.92 GBP Price must be between £1.49 and £7.81.	70%	£0.03	£1.32
Amazon.de	☑ Set DE price automatically based on US price €2.60	70%	€0.03	€1.80
Amazon.fr	☑ Set FR price automatically based on US price €2.60	70%	€0.03	€1.80
	☑ Set ES price automatically			

Step 7: Set the prices for different countries.

5. Click Save and Continue.

6. Choose the territories where you want your e-book to be available. Note that different royalty rates may apply for different countries, depending on whether your book is enrolled in KDP Select or not.

7. Choose the price for your e-book in all countries, or allow Amazon to convert the US price into each individual currency.

8. Read the terms and conditions, and then check the box.

9. Click Save and Publish.

Hot Tip

Make sure that you look at your KDP file in the previewer before you publish and that you are aware of how it appears on all the various devices.

Your Book's Page

After you have uploaded to the KDP platform, your book should go live within 12 hours. This means that it will be for sale on all Amazon websites, and your title will have its own dedicated book page where users can read the description, view a sample, make a purchase and download the e-book to their Kindles or other e-reading devices.

Making Changes

If at any time you wish to make changes to your e-book (e.g. price, metadata, etc.), or if you want to upload an amended e-book file or new cover, simply click on the title on the KDP

Bookshelf page, make your changes and resubmit. You can also unpublish and view the book's individual product pages on each Amazon website by checking the box next to the title and using the Actions button.

TRACKING AMAZON SALES

On the KDP homepage, the Reports tab gives you access to all the information you need in order to track sales and royalties.

- **Month-to-Date Unit Sales**: See how many books you have sold that month in each Amazon territory. Use the drop-down menu to change countries.

- **Prior Six Weeks' Royalties**: See how much you have earned for each title over the previous six weeks. This report is updated every Sunday.

#	Title	ASIN	Units Sold	Units Refunded	Net Units Sold	Units Borrowed*
1	Larvae	B00D9V3AMC	2	0	2	0
2	Murder L	B00CVBOSWW	69	2	67	9
3	Rogues	B00DNFY7DK	12	0	12	0
4	The Channel Swim	B00D9WY3CC	0	0	0	0
5	The Conning Tower	B00D9VHH0S	19	0	19	1
6	The Eynhallow Enmity	B00ASE9SBU	55	1	54	2
7	The Loch	B00CR1E5ME	27	1	26	2
8	The Pack	B00D9WKAOC	1	0	1	0

View report for: Amazon.com

Search [ ] GO View all

Amazon.com
Amazon.co.uk
Amazon.de
Amazon.fr
Amazon.es
Amazon.it
Amazon.co.jp
Amazon.in
Amazon.ca
Amazon.com.br
Amazon.com.mx
Amazon.com.au

Unit sales coverin___ 0/31/2013

Month-to-date uni___ 1/01/2013 to 11/15/2013

Above: You can view the sales reports of your books in different countries.

- **Prior Months' Royalties**: You can download your monthly sales and royalties in XLS format. These files are made available on the 15th of each month.

- **Promotions**: Control KDP Select promotions, such as free giveaways and Countdown Deals (more on this in chapter six).

- **Sales Dashboard**: Provides a graph for daily sales of all or specific titles over any given period and marketplace.

Payment and Remittance Advice

Amazon will also send you an email once a month detailing your earnings. However, all sales on KDP are paid 60 days in arrears, so you will have to wait two months for your first payment.

Above: Simply enter an email address and password to sign up for Kobo.

KOBO WRITING LIFE

Kobo provides e-books to several high street retailers, such as WH Smith in the UK. In addition, it is very popular in Canada and Australia, so it is worthwhile taking advantage of its self-publishing platform Writing Life. Of course, most aggregators will distribute your book to Kobo, but Writing Life is simple to use, and going directly there means that you can receive 70 per cent royalties (for books priced above £1.99 or $1.99) rather than the 60 per cent offered by Smashwords and other aggregators.

Signing Up

Kobo requires just an email address and password to sign up. After this, you can begin uploading your books. Kobo books are sold in ePub format, so you can upload your own ePub files, or a .doc, Mobi, HTML, PDF or text file, which the platform will convert for you.

Uploading to Kobo

1. After signing in to Kobo, click E-Books in the top right-hand corner.

2. Click the green Create New E-Book tab.

3. Enter the metadata for your book, including title, author name, categories and description.

> ## Hot Tip
> Make sure that you read the terms and conditions before uploading your e-book to Kobo, especially if your novel contains adult content, as they are very strict on the type of books they permit on their site.

4. Upload your e-book cover by clicking the rectangular cover placeholder, and then click 'Save and next'.

5. Upload your content using the green Upload button. Kobo will then convert your file into an ePub.

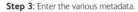

DESCRIBE THE eBOOK

eBook title
Rogues

eBook sub-title
optional

Series name
optional

Author(s)
Robert Forrester   Add another author

Publisher name
Best of Both Worlds

Imprint
optional

Publication date

ROBERT
FORRESTER

ROGUES
Elephants Never Forget...

Describe your eBook
Add eBook content ✓
Choose content rights ✓
Set the price ✓
Publish your eBook

Save and next
Save and stop editing

Step 3: Enter the various metadata.

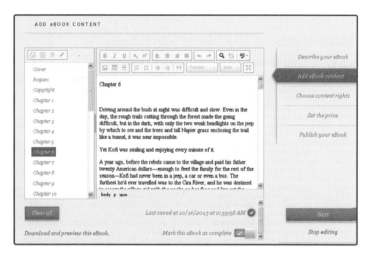

Above: Kobo still allows you to edit an e-book file after it has been uploaded.

Editing Your Kobo ePub

One of the best features of Kobo's Writing Life is the ability to edit the e-book content once you have uploaded it. Simply click the blue Edit This Book tab to begin. Make sure that you check the table of contents for the correct chapter titles and headings.

Rights and Pricing

Once you have finished editing your title, click Next. You will then be asked to confirm worldwide rights and whether or not to add DRM (Digital Rights Management; *see* page 93). After clicking 'Save and next', you can set the prices for each territory before going on to publish your e-book.

Kobo Dashboard

The Dashboard tab in Writing Life lets you see all of your sales information, such as sales for each title, monthly sales, total sales and royalties earned.

NOOK PRESS

Barnes & Noble's first attempt at a self-publishing platform, Pubit, which was only available for those in the USA, has now been discontinued, but they have replaced it with Nook Press, which is available to non-US authors too. All you need to begin is an e-mail address.

Uploading to Nook Press

You can upload .doc, HTML or ePub files of your e-book to the Nook Press platform. In order to begin, simply click the Manuscript File tab. After uploading your e-book, you can enter all your metadata and pricing information, and upload a cover image using the dashboard on the left. Once complete, click the Publish tab in the top right-hand corner.

Upload Your File

You can upload a Microsoft Word (.doc/.docx), .txt, .rtf, .htm, .html, or .epub manuscript file. Once uploaded, you can edit the text in the Manuscript Editor, invite collaborators to read your Manuscript, and preview the NOOK Book as it will appear on NOOK.

For best results, format your file according to our guidelines: doc/docx, txt, html, epub

Choose File

File to Upload: Rogues Kindle.doc
File Type: Microsoft Word Document

Cancel   Create Project

Above: Click the Manuscript File tab and choose the file to be uploaded.

Nook Royalties and Sales

Nook Press pays 65 per cent royalties on e-books, and you can view your sales and royalties by clicking the Monthly Sales Reports button. You can also bring up a sales graph that shows the number of books sold, or your net royalties over a six-month or one-year period.

iBOOK STORE

Until recently, in order to get an e-book for sale on the iBook Store, you needed to go through an aggregator, such as Smashwords, because Apple had particular requirements on how it wanted e-books formatted.

Hot Tip

Nook Press is fairly new and some authors have experienced teething problems, such as their chapters not being separated properly. Use the Edit Manuscript facility to check and make changes to your file before publishing.

However, the company has now introduced iBooks Author, which lets authors format their e-books and upload them directly to the iBook Store. You can download iBooks Author from the Apple App Store, and it comes with an easy-to-use interface and guide to walk you through the process.

OTHER RETAILERS

Most other major e-book retailers do not have the facilities to self-publish directly, so you will have to use an aggregator such as Smashwords if you want your books listed on the Sony Reader Store, Diesel eBook Store and Flipkart.

OTHER DISTRIBUTION OPTIONS

E-book retailers are not the only places where you can sell your novel, as there are other options for self-published authors.

Selling on Your Own Website

If you have a popular blog or website, you can use this platform to sell your e-book directly to people. If you host your e-book on your website and use payment systems such as PayPal, you will not have to pay royalties to anybody else for e-book downloads.

Intermediary Services

If you do not have your own blog or website but you still want a place to host your e-book without having to pay the royalty rates charged by the main online retailers, you can use one of several intermediary services:

- **Payhip:** Provides a platform and the payment facilities to sell your e-book directly to readers. They charge five per cent on each transaction.

- **Click2Sell:** Lets you upload and sell e-books on their affiliate marketing platform.

- **E-junkie:** A simple alternative that lets you sell your book in PDF format.

Hot Tip

Remember that, unlike printed books, e-books are subject to sales tax in certain countries, so you may have to register with the tax authorities.

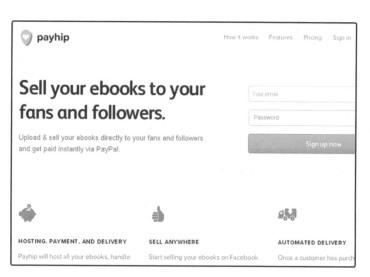

Above: Payhip is an intermediary service that allows you to sell directly to readers.

PRINT ON DEMAND

While e-books make it easier to distribute and sell books to readers, there is nothing like having your own physical copy of your novel, and print on demand (POD) has made hard copy books much more affordable to produce.

HOW DOES POD WORK?

Self-publishing your own printed book used to be costly. Printers required a minimum print run of hundreds or even thousands of copies, which you had to pay for in advance, thus making self-publishing out of reach for many people. However, print on demand has changed all that. Thanks to digital technology, you upload your book file and a book is only printed when somebody orders a copy. Furthermore, the price of printing is added straight to the cover price, so an author or publisher does not have to pay the printing costs.

POD Costs

The big advantage of print on demand is that it costs hardly anything to upload your book to a POD service. While some POD publishers charge a setup fee, this is normally quite small and you only have to pay it once, no matter how many books end up being printed.

WHY PRINT?

The majority of self-published authors sell very few print titles compared to e-books. However, having a print version of your e-book can bring plenty of benefits.

Marketing

A printed book provides a useful marketing tool. You can use print editions for signings at local bookshops, libraries and events, which is a great way to build a platform in your local community. Printed books are also great for sending out as review copies. While there are plenty of e-book review sites on the internet, having a hard-copy edition enables you to approach those magazines and websites that do not accept e-books.

Reach

Having a printed book also means that you can reach those readers who have yet to adopt digital e-reading technology or simply prefer physical copies. Additionally, a print edition listed alongside your e-book makes the latter's price look more attractive.

Hot Tip

If you have a print version, Amazon will list the price on your e-book page and show readers how much money they save on the e-book edition.

Right: Amazon displays the price of the printed book alongside the e-book price. and points out the savings on an e-book.

POD PUBLISHERS

You will find that there are numerous POD publishers available, and each has its own strengths when it comes to book publishing and distribution.

○ **CreateSpace**: Owned by Amazon, CreateSpace has no setup costs and you get automatic distribution to Amazon. You can also opt for expanded distribution, enabling you to reach other retailers.

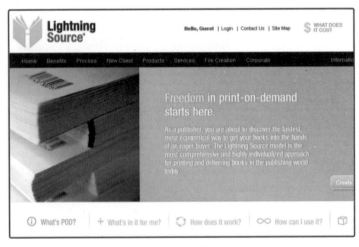

Above: Lightning Source demands a small fee, but distributes widely.

○ **Lightning Source**: While a small setup fee is required, Lightning Source distributes to all retailers, libraries and academic institutions.

○ **Lulu**: An easy-to-use service, its basic print editions do not cost anything to produce or distribute through the Lulu Marketplace.

○ **Blurb**: Better known for full-colour photography books, Blurb also has a couple of black-and-white text novel options.

ISBN Services

Most of these POD services provide distribution services, but in order for retailers to order and stock your title, you will need an ISBN. Some platforms charge you for this, whereas others, such as CreateSpace, will provide you with one for free, although this does mean CreateSpace or whichever POD company you use will be listed as the publisher.

DISADVANTAGES OF POD

While POD has enabled many self-published authors to get their work into print, it does come with its problems.

Unit Price

The cost of POD books per unit is higher than that for books produced through a traditional print run. This means that self-published authors may find that they cannot price their books as competitively as they can with their e-books, thus making it harder to compete with traditionally published books.

Above: POD services may end up providing low royalties.

Costs and Royalties

As the cover price has to include the production costs and the retailer's commission, POD books can be expensive for consumers and provide very low royalties to authors.

Production

Creating a professional and high-quality printed book is not easy. Formatting and designing a printed book is an art form in itself, and producing a book that can compete with traditionally published novels is extremely difficult and time-consuming.

Hot Tip

A POD book priced at $14.99 (£10.99) may yield less than $3.00 (£2.00) in royalties if sold through an online store, and much less if sold through other retailers.

EXPANDED DISTRIBUTION

Although you can attach an ISBN to your POD book, this does not mean that you will see your work on the shelves of your local bookshop. Expanded POD distribution programmes allow your book to be listed in the distribution catalogues and online databases used by bookstores, but unless you become very successful, bookshops are unlikely to stock your titles, as they tend to go for well-known names or recommendations from publications such as *Publishers Weekly*. However, they may order a copy for someone if it is requested.

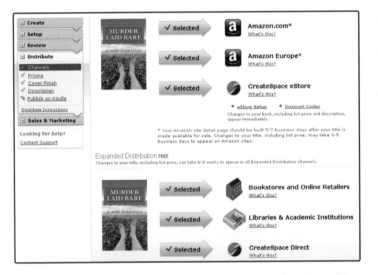

Above: CreateSpace now offers free expanded distribution, which used to cost $25.

Amazon

CreateSpace pays the highest royalties of all the main POD publishers, but using them to get your book printed has its problems. Even if you go on to become a bestseller, you may find that retailers refuse to stock your book. This is because of the dominance that Amazon has in the book retail industry, which has caused many bookshops to refuse to stock their products, including CreateSpace books. However, with other services, there is no such issue.

Wholesale Discounts

While your POD book may earn you royalties when sold through online retailers such as Amazon, the size of discount that retailers expect means that you may make very little on each copy sold in a retail store. If you opt for CreateSpace, the company will set the discount rate, but Lightning Source allows you to set your own and, in order to attract retailers, you will need to set it quite high.

Returns

Another problem when trying to sell books through traditional bookshops is the returns system. Most bookshops expect to be able to return a book if it does not sell within a certain time frame, and without this option, they are unlikely to stock it. The only POD publisher that enables returns is Lightning Source; if a book is returned, the money is deducted from your monthly royalties.

Hot Tip

In order to take advantage of the higher online royalties, some self-published authors use CreateSpace for Amazon distribution and another POD programme, such as Lightning Source, for other distribution channels.

DISTRIBUTING THROUGH CREATESPACE

If you wish to produce a printed book and sell it through online stores, such as Amazon, CreateSpace is the best option because of its higher royalty rate.

1. Join CreateSpace by registering at www.createspace.com.

2. Click on the New Title button to upload your book and create your POD title.

3. Follow the online prompts; choose your trim size and include the metadata for your book.

Step 3: Enter the metadata for your book.

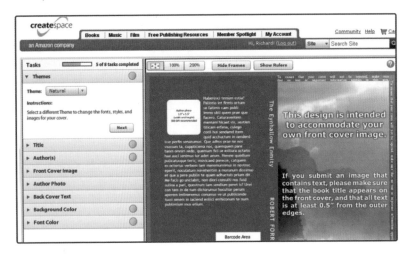

Step 4: CreateSpace offers a cover creator tool.

4. Upload your formatted book in either .doc or PDF format, and then upload or create your own cover using the CreateSpace cover creator.

5. Complete the setup process and submit for review.

Review and Proofs

Your book will be reviewed manually, and CreateSpace will email you about any problems. Once the book has gone through the review process, you can order proofs before you submit the title for distribution. These can be either in PDF (free) or a hard copy (at cost price, usually around $5.00, plus post and packaging).

DISTRIBUTING THROUGH LIGHTNING SOURCE

Lightning Source is perhaps the best option for distributing to non-Amazon retailers, libraries and other distribution channels.

1. After signing up for a new account at www1.lightningsource.com, select the My Library header at the top of the page and choose Setup A New Title from the drop-down menu.

2. Enter the metadata, including ISBN, title and contributor, and then click Save.

3. Enter the returnable status, bind type, publication date, page count and price for your book. Click Save when finished.

4. Upload your cover and interior files, and choose whether you want to receive a proof.

5. Check all the information you have entered and if everything is correct click Go. On the next screen, click I Agree to the terms and conditions in order to submit your file for review.

Hot Tip

Lightning Source charges a one-off setup fee of $37.50 (£23) and $30 (£19) for proofs (including post and packaging). You also have to pay for any revisions to your POD book.

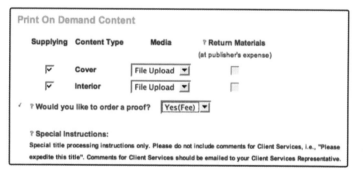

Step 3: Fill in the fields, including information such as publication date and page count.

Step 4: Upload the cover and interior files.

MARKETING & SOCIAL MEDIA

MARKETING YOUR BOOK

Writing and distributing your e-book is only the first step to self-publishing. In order to build up an audience and make sales, you will need to reach out to readers, and that means marketing your novel.

DISCOVERY

Once they have written and distributed their book through various online retailers, one of the biggest disappointments many self-published authors face is when it fails to sell many copies. No matter how great the novel, an unknown author cannot expect readers to stumble upon their title among the hundreds of thousands of other e-books available in online stores. This is why, if you want readers to discover your e-book, you are going to have to spend some time promoting it.

Above: Low sales can be discouraging, but a good marketing plan can help boost sales.

MARKETING PLAN

Book promotion can be daunting, especially for new authors or those with no marketing experience, but the simplest way to approach it is to come up with a marketing plan on how best to reach out to readers and generate interest in your novel.

Planning Your Promotion

Essentially, there are three stages to an e-book marketing plan:

- **Prelaunch:** There is no point in waiting until your book is released before you begin promotion; you need to drum up interest in your novel long before it is launched.

- **Launch:** If you come up with a firm launch date, you can plan promotions to coincide with it.

- **Post-launch:** The work never stops. You will need to continue to market you novel in order to build up your audience.

LAUNCH DATE

Having a firm release date for your book enables you to plan your promotions around the launch. You need to ensure that you have plenty of time to arrange reviews and generate interest in your book. All your prelaunch marketing should focus on the release date, so that when your book is finally launched, you can start building up an audience straightaway.

Hot Tip

Book sales tend to slow down in the summer, whereas the two months preceding Christmas are very busy for book launches, so choose a date carefully.

Book contributors: (What's this?)
Robert Forrester (Author)

Add contributors

Language (What's this?)
English

Publication date (optional)

	Nov	2013				
Mo	**Tu**	**We**	**Th**	**Fr**	**Sa**	**Su**
				1	2	3
4	5	6	7	8	9	10
11	12	13	14	15	16	17
18	19	20	21	22	23	24
25	26	27	28	29	30	

ISBN (optional) (What's this?)

2. Verify Your Publishing Ri

Verify Your Publishing Rights (What's this?)
- ○ This is a public domain work.
- ⊙ This is not a public domain work and I hold the necessary publishing rights.

3. Target Your Book to Customers

Categories (What's this?)

FICTION > Thrillers > Suspense
FICTION > Short Stories

Above: Choose a publication date and plan promotions around it.

PRELAUNCH PROMOTION

You should begin marketing your book long before it is released. Plan your marketing at least a year ahead, even if you are still writing your novel. Start reaching out to potential readers and like-minded people who may be interested in your work. Search the internet for readers' groups, book clubs and other forums where you might find potential readers. Engage with people and explain what your book is about.

SOCIAL MEDIA

Social media networks can be powerful tools for book promotion and we will explore how to use them to build an author platform in the next section. If you are not on the most popular social media platforms, make sure that you sign up long before you release your book.

- **Twitter:** With over half a billion users, Twitter is a great place to promote your book, build a readership and network with other writers.

Above: Goodreads is a social media platform dedicated to literature.

- **Facebook:** Allows you to create an author page, where you can publicize your book and get people excited about it.

- **Goodreads:** A social media platform designed solely around books, readers and authors.

PLANNING YOUR RELEASE

Once you have established a release date for your book and begun seeking out potential readers, you need to target websites that will promote your book – and this means seeking reviews.

BOOK REVIEWS

No matter how great your novel, if it is self-published, there is little chance of mainstream publications reviewing it. For self-published authors, the best option for getting a book reviewed is to approach book bloggers. However, competition is stiff and you may have to send your book to dozens of different book review blogs; here are some of the more popular ones.

Above: Try to get your book reviewed by a popular book review blog such as IndieReader.

- **BigAl's Books & Pals**: Reviews e-books by independent authors (www.booksandpals.blogspot.com).

- **IndieReader**: A popular independent book review blog (www.indiereader.com).

- **The Indie View**: Has links to independent book reviewers and hosts its own book reviews (www.theindieview.com).

Hot Tip

Kirkus (www.kirkusreviews .com), the long-standing book review publication, now has a self-published section, but you do have to pay from $425 (£260) to have your book reviewed.

Getting Your Book Reviewed

Asking for reviews can be quite daunting for the first-time author, but many book bloggers make the process easy. Most bloggers will have guidelines on their blog for submitting your e-book for review, which you should follow precisely. You will most likely have to send a free copy of your e-book in a specified format, along with a cover image, a description of the book and a brief biography of yourself. Avoid sending the same email to dozens of different book bloggers. Instead, write each request individually and address the blogger by name.

Above: Try not to react badly to negative reviews, especially as some may offer constructive criticism.

Above: Biased comments from people you know are usually against the review guidelines set out on websites.

Handling Criticism

When it comes to reviews, you need to prepare for negative comments, as not everybody is going to like your book. Pay attention to any constructive criticism that may improve your book or help you to develop as a writer. Although you may not agree with some of the comments made, never get into a debate with a reviewer, as this could result in an argument and you may risk coming across as unprofessional.

Customer Reviews

Before your book is released, it is a good idea to give away copies to people interested in reading it in an attempt to get reviews on websites such as Amazon and Goodreads. However, refrain from handing it out for friends and family to review, as biased comments are easily spotted and are against the review guidelines set down by most websites. It is also a good idea to ask reviewers to make it clear in their review that they were given a free copy in exchange for unbiased feedback.

BLOGGING

If you already have a blog or website, make sure that you take advantage of this platform to promote your book. Of course, you do not want to overdo it and risk annoying your existing blog audience, but few people will mind the odd post about your novel.

Hot Tip

If you do not have a blog, consider starting one. You can talk about the process of writing your book, include excerpts of your novel and even review books by other authors.

Blog Tours

Before, when authors released a book, their only choice was to rack up miles and miles doing signings at bookshops and libraries. These days, thanks to the internet, you can reach readers without leaving your home. Blog tours are an effective way of promotion, but can be just as much hard work, as they involve contacting bloggers for reviews and interviews and submitting guest posts. They do have to be planned well in advance and you should begin contacting bloggers two or three months before your book is scheduled for release.

Mailing List and Links

If you have a blog or website, think about setting up a mailing list. Having a list of email addresses of people who might be interested in buying your book can help you to generate sales early on. In addition, when your book is released, make sure that you include links to it on your website, blog and Facebook page in order to make it easy for people to find it.

PRE-ORDERS

One marketing strategy that is worth considering is using pre-orders. Not all online retailers permit it, but pre-ordering enables you to list your book before its official release date. Customers can view the product description, read a sample and place an order, but they cannot actually download the book until the official release date.

Pre-ordering offers several benefits, including the following:

Hot Tip

Smashwords' pre-ordering system lets you list your book on Apple, Barnes & Noble and Kobo several weeks before its official release date.

- **Advance marketing**: You will already have a product page to which you can link in your marketing campaigns.

- **Estimate sales**: Pre-ordering lets you estimate how well your book will sell when it actually goes on sale.

Left: Smashwords allows you to list your book on vendors' websites before it is released.

- **Marketing effectiveness**: You can judge how effective your marketing is and make changes before your book goes live.

- **Rankings**: You can appear in bestseller lists and acquire book rankings, providing higher visibility for when your book finally goes on sale.

MARKETING STRATEGIES

When your book is finally released, your marketing strategies need to move up a gear. Making those early sales can be quite difficult, especially for an unknown author without a platform. However, many of the online retailers offer several tools to help you get noticed.

NEW RELEASES

Most online retailers offer extra exposure for newly released books. Usually, this is a dedicated category in which newly released books are listed. However, Amazon provides two different new-release categories:

- **Last 30 Days**: A listing for books released in the last 30 days.

- **Last 90 Days**: Books released in the last three months.

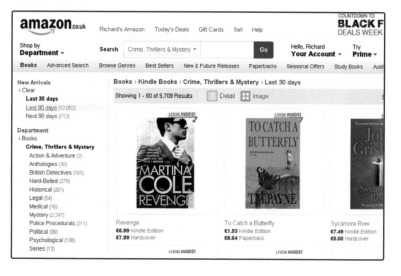

Right: Amazon highlights books released in the last month, and the last three months.

Early Sales

Most new-release categories list the newest books first. This often means that authors find they sell quite a few books early on, but then sales tend to slow as the book ages. This is because books drop down the new-release categories and become less visible, making it harder for readers to stumble upon them.

RECOMMENDATIONS

Recommendation engines can be powerful marketing tools. Most online retailers provide recommendations at the bottom of a book's product page to help customers find similar titles to the one they are looking at. Even if you have not sold any copies, some of these recommendation engines will link books together, based on page views, product descriptions, keywords or other metadata.

Hot Tip

If you do a discount promotion or giveaway as soon as your book is released, it helps it to appear on the also-viewed and recommendation listings, which can improve visibility.

Email Recommendations

Another great marketing tool provided by the main online retailers is the emails they send out to customers. People who buy books are often sent emails with other book recommendations, meaning that customers can discover your title without even having to visit the online store.

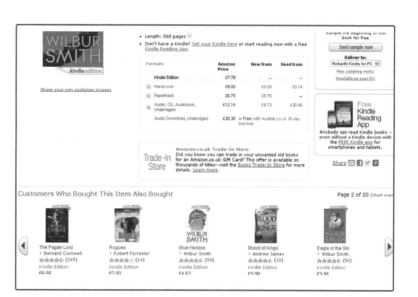

Above: Online retailers often give recommendations based on what a user has bought previously.

Buying Habits

Most online retailers also tailor recommendations based on a customer's personal buying habits, usually offering a list of books on the individual's homepage, according to the types of titles that they have bought before.

KDP SELECT

Amazon has a unique marketing programme available for KDP authors called KDP Select, which offers several benefits:

- **Free promotions**: Authors in the Select program can offer their book free for up to five days in every 90-day period.

- **Countdown deals**: Select authors can provide a timed discount that is visible to readers on the product page.

- **Paid borrows**: Readers enrolled in Amazon's Prime program can borrow an e-book for free each month, and Amazon pays authors in the Select program between $2–$3 for each of these borrows.

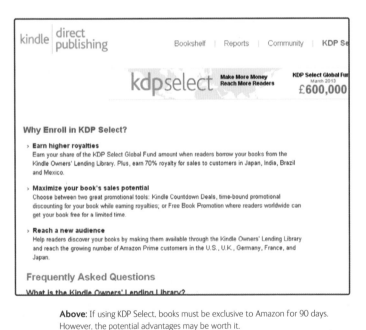

Above: If using KDP Select, books must be exclusive to Amazon for 90 days. However, the potential advantages may be worth it.

Exclusivity

The main disadvantage of the KDP Select program is that you have to offer the e-book exclusively to Amazon for 90 days, and therefore cannot have it listed with any other online retailer. You cannot even offer it for sale on your own blog or website. As Amazon is by far the largest marketplace for independent authors, the paid-for borrows and added marketing tools may be worth the exclusivity, but this will depend on how many books you sell on other websites.

DISCOUNTS AND FREE PROMOTIONS

Although you may have spent a long time working out the best price for your e-book, offering discounted or even free e-books can be an effective marketing strategy.

- **Exposure**: More readers will download your book if it is free or discounted, thus offering you added visibility in recommendation engines and category listings.

- **Platform**: Giving away free and discounted books means that more people will read them, and those who enjoy them may buy your next book.

- **Charts**: Retailers such as Amazon and Smashwords have bestseller lists for free and discounted titles, offering you added exposure.

- **Reviews**: If people download your book, you are more likely to receive customer reviews.

- **Cross-selling**: If you have several titles for sale, giveaways and discounts can encourage people to buy your other books.

Hot Tip

Smashwords offers coupon codes so you can offer free or discounted titles to people with the code but keep your book listed at its usual price.

Right: Generate a coupon to offer your books for free or a discount on Smashwords.

DISADVANTAGES OF PRICE PROMOTIONS

Free promotions and discounts are not without their drawbacks.

- **Reading**: Just because people have downloaded your free book, it does not necessarily mean that they will read it. Some people download dozens of free titles but never get around to reading them.

- **Audience**: If you have written a niche title, by giving your book away for free or at a discounted rate, you risk diminishing the size of the audience who would have paid full price for it.

- **Readership**: People who may not normally like your type of novel may still download it if it is free or discounted. This can lead to negative reviews if they do not enjoy it.

- **Expectation**: Readers who have downloaded discounted or free titles may expect your other titles to be the same price.

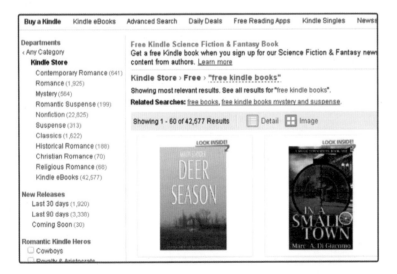

Effective Promotion

Many self-published authors have found that free promotions and heavily discounted books are not as effective for marketing as they used to be. Primarily, this is because of the number of free and discounted titles continuously available at

Left: So many people offer free promotions that it is no longer the effective marketing strategy it used to be.

many online stores. However, other authors continue to do well using this strategy. With any form of promotion, it is important to remember that what may be effective for one author may not necessarily be right for another.

ADVANCED MARKETING STRATEGIES

The great thing about self-publishing is that it gives you the freedom to try new things. This means that you can experiment with your marketing and find innovative ways to reach readers.

Serials

Since e-books do not have any print or distribution costs attached to their production, you do not have to release an entire novel in one go. Some authors have found success by serializing their books, offering monthly instalments. This gives you the ability to discount early editions, and if customers like what they have read, they may buy the next instalment. In addition, serializing a book means that you will have more visibility, as each instalment will have its own product page, and you will always have something new to promote and discuss on social media. Furthermore, by splitting a novel into several sections, even if you price each instalment low, you can get a better accumulative return.

> ## Hot Tip
>
> If you serialize a novel, once you have released the final instalment, compile them all into a single e-book and price it a little lower than the combined cost of each separate instalment.

Above: Amazon has a specific programme for serial e–books called Kindle Serials.

Above: Quote excerpts from your novel on social media to generate interest.

Excerpts/Teasers

If you have a blog, website or Facebook page, a good way to generate a buzz and get readers interested in your book is to post excerpts and teasers. These can just be the first few chapters, or you can serialize your entire novel on your website, thus encouraging those people who cannot wait for the next instalment to buy the book. Even though it has a 140-character limit, you can still use Twitter in this way. Try tweeting sentences, such as the opening line to your novel, which can intrigue or hook your followers so that they will want to read more.

LOCAL MARKETING

Despite the rise of social media and online bookstores that can get your novel seen by people all over the planet, marketing in your local area and to your friends and family is still an effective way to start your author platform. Word of mouth is by far the most effective promotional tool, but it has to start somewhere, so make sure that you let your friends and family know that you have written a novel.

Local Events

As a self-published author, you may not be able to do a world book tour to promote your novel, but that does not mean that you cannot hold events in your local area. If you have a printed version of your book, speak to your local independent bookshop and see if they are willing to let you do a signing, or ask at the library if you can hold a reading or book launch. You can advertise these events by handing out leaflets in your area or putting an advert in the local paper.

ONGOING PROMOTION

Even after your book has been out for a while and you begin selling copies, your marketing should not stop. Building your platform involves reaching out to new readers in order to expand your audience, which means that you need to keep on promoting.

ADVERTISING

As a self-published author, you may not be able to afford to advertise your book in the national press or on billboards, but plenty of places are available where you can publicize your novel and reach out to new readers.

- www.bookbub.com: A daily email that goes to over a million book lovers.

Above: BookBub is the most popular website for promoting free or discounted e-books.

BookBub charges to advertise discounted or free e-books, and has strict selection criteria and rejects more books than it accepts.

- **addictedtoebooks.com**: Has both free and paid-for advertising, but all e-books have to be priced below $5.99 (£3.70).

- **bargainebookhunter.com**: Offers free advertising for books on free promotions, as well as paid-for advertising for books priced below $5 (£3).

- **digitalbooktoday.com**: A popular e-book website that offers advertising and sponsorship opportunities for self-published authors.

MONITORING YOUR SUCCESS

As promotion and marketing take time and effort, you need to know whether they are effective. Therefore, you need to monitor your sales and analytics in order to see what is working and what is not.

Book Analytics

If you have a blog or website, make sure that you keep track of page views and any direct downloads. Although most online retailers do not provide authors with much data other than sales figures, Smashwords gives analytics for page views and the number of samples downloaded, which can be useful when you are promoting your e-book on their website.

Tracking Sales

Perhaps the most obvious way to understand the effectiveness of your marketing is by monitoring your sales. Make sure that you keep regular track of them, especially if you are running a discount or free promotion. Try to spot any trends, such as whether discounting your e-book increases the number of other titles that you sell.

Above: Keep a spreadsheet recording your sales to track the effectiveness of your promotions.

OVERPROMOTION

Few people start writing fiction because they are interested in promotion. For most authors, marketing is a necessary evil, but it can be all too easy to neglect your writing by spending too much time promoting your novel. Overdoing promotion, particularly on social media, can annoy people – especially if all you talk about is your book – and it can also be counterproductive.

Writing as Promotion

While promoting your first book is important in order to build an initial audience, writing another book is by far the best way to create an author platform. The more novels you write, the more visibility you will have. In addition, people who bought and enjoyed the first book may buy the next, and those who have only bought the second book may go on to buy the first. As spending too much time on marketing and promotion takes time away from writing, you need to strike a balance: dedicate just a small portion of your free time to promotion and the rest to putting words on the page.

Hot Tip

Look online or in the local paper to see if there are reading groups or book clubs in your area which you could contact offering copies of your book for their discussions.

YOUR AUTHOR PLATFORM

As an author, you need visibility and the ability to reach readers. This is your author platform, but building it is not easy and requires more than just promotion.

DEFINING AUTHOR PLATFORM

Before you can build an author platform, it is important that you understand what one is and how it can help you to build an audience.

- **Reach:** The number of people who buy and read your books is perhaps the most fundamental aspect of any writer's author platform.

○ **Visibility:** Your author platform is how visible you are. Authors with lots of books in numerous venues have high visibility, but new authors with just one or two books listed do not.

○ **Reputation:** What you are known for writing, such as your genre, is very much part of your author platform.

○ **Audience:** The sorts of people who will buy your books are also part of your author platform. Certain types of books often appeal to people in certain demographics.

Hot Tip

If you have an existing platform, such as a popular blog or being well known for something else, you can use this as a foundation for your author platform.

BUILDING AN AUTHOR PLATFORM

An author platform grows from your work. An author who just releases one book cannot expect to attract lots of readers straightaway (although it can happen). In order to build a platform, you will need to keep on writing and build up a body of work. However, simply churning out title after title will not necessarily help with your author platform either, as you need to produce good-quality books that people will want to read. Building an author platform takes a lot of time and effort.

TARGET AUDIENCE

To build up an author platform, you need to reach your audience. First of all, you need to establish where to find your potential readers. Your audience may be quite diverse, or quite gender or age specific, such as teens and young adults. Once you have identified who your readers are, you need to base your platform around them.

● **Book distribution:** You need to distribute your books where your readers will find them. While online stores are great for reaching large numbers of people, if you write in a particular niche, you may find better places to reach your readers.

Left: Identify your readers, for example, young adults, and tailor your marketing approach to them.

- **Communication**: You need to find the best place to reach out to your readers. This may be a particular group on social media, or it may involve using another method, such as blog tours or events.

- **Writing**: You need to write books that your readers will want to read. Swapping genre or style can alienate your existing readers.

Communicating with Your Audience

Many authors make the mistake of thinking that building an author platform is just about promoting their work. However, constant marketing of your books will soon annoy people. The best method of communicating with readers is to engage with them about the genre as a whole, so talk about other books and media related to your work.

SOCIAL MEDIA

Social media offers authors fantastic opportunities to reach out to their audience, and therefore having a social media presence is crucial for all new writers. Social media enables you to engage with potentially millions of readers who may share and discuss your work with their friends and followers. The best social media tools for authors include the following:

- **Facebook**: With over a billion users, Facebook is the world's most popular social media platform.

Right: Facebook is a key social media platform for promotion, as it is so popular.

Connect with friends and the world around you on Facebook.

See photos and updates from friends in News Feed.

Share what's new in your life on your Timeline.

Find more of what you're looking for with Graph Search.

Sign Up
It's free and always will be.

First Name / Last Name

Your Email

Re-enter Email

New Password

Birthday
Month / Day / Year   Why do I need to provide my birthday?

○ Female ○ Male

By clicking Sign Up, you agree to our Terms and that you have read our Data Use Policy, including our Cookie Use.

Sign Up

- **Twitter**: A simple and easy way to engage with readers, as well as promoting your work.

- **Goodreads**: A social media platform where everybody is interested in reading and books.

Step 2: Click the Create Page link.

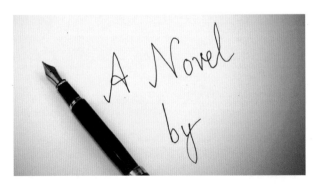

FACEBOOK FOR AUTHORS

Facebook can be a valuable tool when building an author platform simply because of the sheer number of people who use it. If you already have a Facebook page, you can use the same account, but it is best to set up a dedicated fan page where you can discuss and promote your book:

1. If you do not have a Facebook account, simply visit www.facebook.com and sign up.

2. At the bottom of your Facebook homepage, click the Create Page link to start a fan page.

3. Choose 'Artist, Band or Public Figure', and then select Author in the drop-down menu.

4. Choose a name for your fan page (preferably your author name) and then check the box to say that you agree with the terms and conditions.

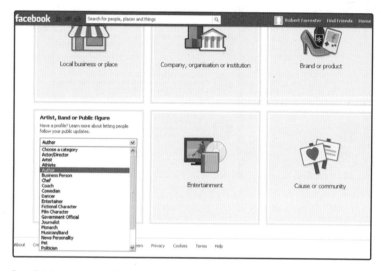

5. Create your page and remember to include links to where your books are for sale, as well as a recent author picture, your book's cover and the description.

Step 3: Select Author from the drop-down menu.

USING TWITTER

Twitter is perhaps the simplest social media platform to use. When you follow people, they quite often follow back, thus helping you to build up a platform. You can send links to your books and your Facebook page, as well as announcing new releases. If people like your messages, they may 'retweet' them, thus helping you to reach more people.

Using Twitter and sending tweets is simple:

1. Sign up to Twitter by visiting www.twitter.com. Create your profile by uploading a recent picture and including a short biography.

Hot Tip

Promote your fan page by sharing it with your current Facebook friends and asking them to 'Like' it. If you have a blog, make sure that you put a link to your fan page on your sidebar.

Step 3: You can add a link to your book to your tweet.

2. Follow like-minded people by clicking their name and the Follow button.

3. In order to send a tweet, click the compose box and write your message. If you wish to include a link to your book, paste it in. Do not worry if the link is too large, as Twitter will shorten it so it fits.

4. Press Tweet.

GOODREADS

Goodreads is a social media platform aimed at people who love books. It contains all sorts of groups, often centred on particular genres of books. For this reason, it is the perfect place for authors to connect with their target audience, but in order to get the most out of Goodreads, you really need to create an author page:

1. Sign up to become a Goodreads member by visiting www.goodreads.com.

2. Look for your e-book using the search bar and if you cannot find it, you can add it yourself by clicking 'Add a New Book'. Include your book's details, cover image and metadata.

Step 2: Add your book's details.

3. Once your book is listed, click on the author name to take you to your basic author page. Scroll down to the bottom and click 'Is this you?'

4. Fill in your details to send a request to join the Author Program. After a few days, you should receive an email confirming that your account has been upgraded to author status.

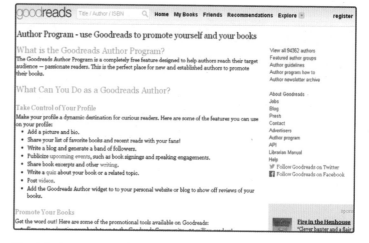

Step 4: Send a request to join the Author Program.

Using Goodreads

Once you have an author account, Goodreads gives you plenty of tools to promote your book to readers:

- **Fans and friends**: You can add friends and become a fan of other authors, while readers can befriend you and become your fans.

- **Share**: You can list your favourite books and recent reads to share with fans and friends.

- **Blog**: You can keep a blog on Goodreads and talk about your work.

- **Publicize**: You can make announcements for upcoming events and book releases. You can even give away books to readers in exchange for reviews.

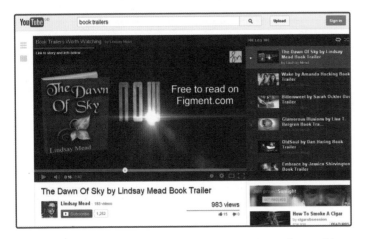

Above: Another way to advertise your book is by uploading a trailer to YouTube.

OTHER SOCIAL MEDIA PLATFORMS

While Facebook, Twitter and Goodreads are the most popular and useful social media platforms for authors, there are others, such as Google+, LinkedIn and Tumblr, which can be useful for reaching readers and your target audience.

YOUR RETAIL PLATFORM

While your e-book will have its own product page on the various online platforms where it is for sale, some of these websites also let you set up an author page. This can be really useful for readers who want to find more books written by you. In addition, your author page can contain other information, such as links to your website and a detailed biography, as well as letting you announce events and new releases.

Hot Tip

Creating a video trailer for your book is a great form of promotion. Use video editing software to create a short advert for your book and upload it to YouTube, the video sharing website.

SMASHWORDS PROFILE

If you are using Smashwords to distribute to various retailers, your profile page will contain information that will be shared with its partner sites. In order to make changes to your author profile, log in to Smashwords and click My Smashwords at the top of the page, where you can add and edit all sorts of information, including:

- **Profile**: Make changes to your profile and edit your author biography.
- **Links**: You can include links to your blog, website, and Facebook and Twitter accounts, as well as places where you can buy any print editions of your title.
- **Interview**: You can write an interview with yourself in a question-and-answer form.

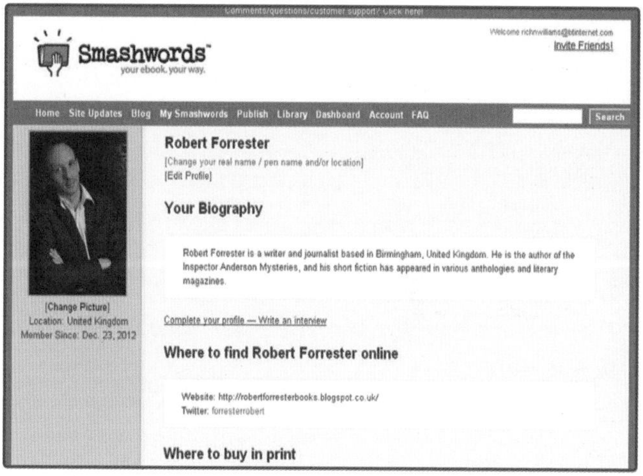

Above: Click Edit Profile to change the information on your Smashwords profile page.

AMAZON AUTHOR CENTRAL

In order to create an author page on Amazon, you first have to join Author Central. This lets you create your author page and make changes to your book's product description, as well as adding editorial reviews and other information. You can also see your e-book's sales rankings, your author ranking and any reviews left by customers.

1. Visit authorcentral.amazon.com to sign in or join up.
2. Click the Books tab at the top to see a list of all your books. If some are missing, you can add them to your author name by clicking the yellow 'Add more books' button.

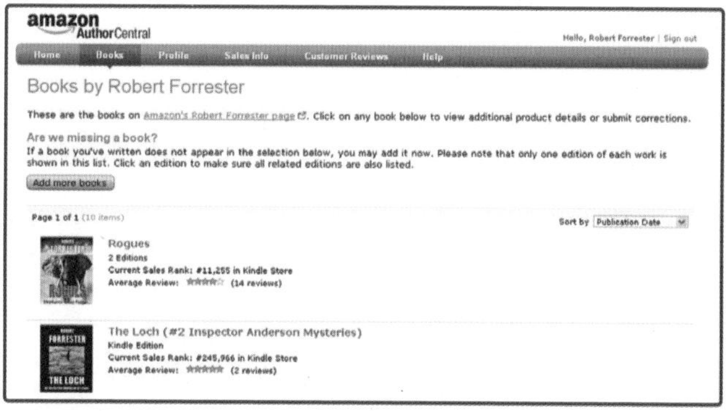

Step 2: Click the Books tab to view the list of all of your books.

Step 3: Click the title of the book you wish to edit, to be taken to that book's specific page.

Step 4: Click the Profile tab to view or edit your profile.

Hot Tip

You need to create separate author pages in both the UK and US versions of Author Central.

3. In order to make changes to your product description, as well as adding editorial reviews and more information about your novel, click the title of your book.

4. In order to add your biography or links to your blog, and to include any special announcements, click the Profile tab at the top of the page.

EXTENDING YOUR INTERNET PLATFORM

These days, readers expect nearly all authors to have their own website. Having a place where you can list all your books, announce new releases and engage with your audience is an important part of building an author platform in the internet age.

Website Options

Creating a website can be time-consuming and expensive, but there are several options. When choosing which type to go for, you need to bear in mind that having your own author name as a web address will come across as more professional than a sub-domain provided by a free platform or third-party host.

- **Bespoke:** Pay somebody to create a bespoke website, which you can host on your own domain. This is the most costly option.

- **Third party:** Cheaper than creating your own website, services such as Godaddy.com or Squarespace.com will host your website, as well as providing you with the tools to create one.

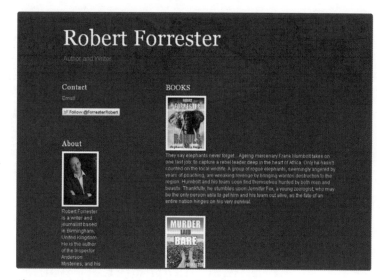

Above: An author website should look professional and offer information and engagement opportunities.

- **Free platforms:** Free services such as Wix.com, Yola.com and Weebly.com provide free hosting and give you the tools to create a website.

BLOGGING

Blogging is a great way to engage more directly with your readers and building up a large audience can really boost your author platform. Even if not all your blog readers buy your books, regular blogging will help to boost your profile and visibility, thus helping you to gain more readers. However, blogging has its disadvantages:

Hot Tip

If you maintain a blog, choose subjects relevant to you as an author, such as books and the genre in which you write.

- **Time**: Blogging requires time. You will need to write new blog posts regularly and also promote your blog.

- **Content**: You have to provide interesting blog posts, rather than just promoting your books. This means that you will have to keep thinking of interesting things to write about.

Above: Sci-fi author John Scalzi has one of the most popular and oldest blogs on the internet.

- **Opinion**: You run the risk of alienating certain readers if you voice your opinions on certain subjects, such as politics or religion.

- **Platform**: It can be just as hard to build a platform for your blog as it is to build an author platform.

PHYSICAL ENGAGEMENT

Even though the internet provides plenty of tools to build an author platform, the old-fashioned method of meeting people face to face is still an effective way to engage with new and existing readers, and there are plenty of ways to do it:

- **Book signings**: Whether in a bookstore or at a local community hall, you can arrange a book-signing event to promote your book in your local area.

- **Talks**: Giving talks at book fairs, reading groups and the local library is a great way to raise your author profile.

- **Writing workshops**: Joining local writers' groups in your area can help you to network with fellow authors and swap advice.

PRESS RELEASES

Although self-published authors rarely get any attention from mainstream publications, local newspapers and periodicals are often more willing to give exposure to authors in their area. When you release your book or organize a local event, send out press releases to the local media. Include a picture of your book cover and your contact details in case they wish to conduct an interview.

Above: Book signings are an excellent way to promote your book.

THE BUSINESS OF SELF-PUBLISHING

COPYRIGHT

Having released your novel in electronic form, you may wonder what is going to stop somebody from copying it. Thankfully, all published work enjoys the same legal protection. It is crucial, therefore, for all authors and publishers to understand copyright in order to protect intellectual property.

INTELLECTUAL PROPERTY

We all know that the law protects the things we own. If somebody takes something that does not belong to them, it is theft. But what happens if somebody takes something that is not physical, such as the content of your book? After all, in today's digital age, it is not difficult to cut and paste words from a page. However, all original artistic

work – whether it is a book, film, piece of music or poem – is known as intellectual property and is automatically protected by copyright from the moment it is produced.

Physical Expression

Copyright protects the physical expression of ideas. In other words, if you simply have some good ideas for a novel, copyright will offer no protection until you express them in written form.

WHAT ISN'T PROTECTED

In the case of a novel, your work is automatically protected by copyright from the moment you put pen to paper. However, copyright does not protect all aspects of your book:

- **Title**: You cannot copyright the title of your novel. Many titles are short and therefore placing them under copyright would prohibit the use of many regular phrases and words.

- **Author name**: People are often born with the same name as somebody else, so you cannot copyright your author name.

- **Ideas**: Copyright only protects the expression of ideas, not the ideas themselves. Therefore, if somebody has written a novel that has a similar story to yours, it is doubtful whether it will be a breach of copyright.

> **Hot Tip**
> Make sure that you keep all the drafts of your work during the different stages, as this can help to prove copyright ownership.

Above: Keep the files of all your manuscript drafts, which will show the dates you worked on them.

COPYRIGHT HOLDER

Copyright protection prevents other people from reproducing, distributing, creating derivative works, selling or lending copyrighted material without permission from the copyright holder. In traditional publishing, authors sell the rights to their copyright (though not the actual copyright of their work) to the publisher. However, most self-published authors tend to retain their rights.

ASSIGNING RIGHTS

When people buy books, they are essentially buying the rights to certain aspects of the copyright. With printed books, a customer owns first sale rights, which means that they can read and even resell that particular copy of the book, but they cannot reproduce it. With e-books, customers have the right to read the content but not to resell, lend or redistribute it.

Within the bordered box:

Robert Forrester

Published internationally by Best of Both Worlds, UK
Park Rd, Birmingham, UK

© Robert Forrester 2013

The right of Robert Forrester to be identified as the author has been asserted in accordance with sections 77 and 78 of the Copyright, Designs and Patents Act 1988. All rights reserved.

Digitally produced by Best of Both Worlds

This book is sold subject to the condition that it shall not, by way of trade or otherwise, be lent, resold, hired out or circulated without the publisher's consent in any form other than this current form and without a similar condition being imposed upon a subsequent purchaser. Any similarity between the characters and situations and places or persons, living or dead, is unintentional and co-incidental.

Chapter One

Above: The copyright page shows who owns the rights.

Distribution Rights

When you sign up to a self-publishing platform, you are assigning rights to the company to distribute your work. In other words, while you remain the copyright holder, the e-book retailers will have the right to sell and distribute your work to whatever territories you have agreed to.

Public Domain

Copyright is not finite. Indeed, copyright protection only lasts for a limited period. With novels, this is often 70 years after the death of the author (although this time limit varies from country to country). Work that is not under copyright is known as public domain, which means that people are free to copy, reproduce and sell it without permission.

Fair Use

In most countries, such as the USA and UK, copyright law allows for certain exceptions. This is known as fair use and means that a limited amount of copyrighted material can be used without permission for purposes such as satire, commentary, criticism, news reporting and education.

Above: Some authors are now allowing fan fiction to be sold on Amazon Worlds, with the royalties split between the rights holder (original author) and the fan fiction writer.

Derivative Works

Fan fiction, i.e. when people write stories based on other popular books and franchises, is very popular, but it can often be a breach of copyright, depending on its use. Many writers of fan fiction claim 'fair use' and most rights holders tolerate it, as long as fan fiction writers do not attempt to sell the work.

Plagiarism

Plagiarism – i.e. when somebody takes the work of somebody else and claims it as their own – is not necessarily a breach of copyright.

If somebody copies the ideas, plot elements and types of character of your novel, but not the actual words, they may not be in breach of copyright, although it can depend on how much they have copied.

Trademarks

Trademarks also differ from copyright. They are names protected by law, which prevents their use in certain circumstances. In fiction, you cannot use trademarked names in your book title, but you can use them in your stories, as long as you do not damage the trademark's reputation. For instance, you can have characters in your story dining in a well-known burger bar, but it might cause legal problems if one of them dies from eating one of the burgers.

COPYRIGHT INFRINGEMENT

When somebody breaches your rights as the copyright holder, it is known as copyright infringement. Examples of copyright infringement include the following:

- **Piracy:** When somebody copies your work and sells it or gives it away free.

- **Plagiarism:** When somebody copies all or part of your work and passes it off as their own.

- **Translation:** Nobody can translate and publish your work in another language without permission.

- **Derivative works:** When people write stories using your characters or base them in a world that you have created.

Copyright Registration

Although all work is automatically protected by copyright, registration of your copyright can make it easier to take action against infringement. Registration of copyright usually involves paying a small fee and sending a copy of the work to the relevant service:

- **UK:** The UK does not have an official copyright register, but companies like www.copyrightservice.co.uk and www.copyrightaid.co.uk offer services such as legal help for those who register.

- **USA:** Registering with the United States Copyright Office (www.copyright.gov) provides you with statutory damages if your copyright is breached.

Above: The USA has an official copyright register.

ENFORCING COPYRIGHT

Copyright infringement is rare, but it can happen. In most cases, copyright infringement is a civil rather than criminal matter, which means that you cannot call the police and have them sort it out for you. Therefore, as a self-published author without the legal department of a big publisher behind you, you have to tackle any copyright infringements on your own.

1. Contact the author, publisher or website where you believe your work has been unlawfully copied and inform them of the violation.

2. If the work is not removed, report the violation to authorities such as search engines, hosting companies, e-book retailers, payment processors and internet service providers (ISPs).

3. If you believe the copyright infringement has resulted in serious financial losses, contact an intellectual property lawyer to file a lawsuit for damages.

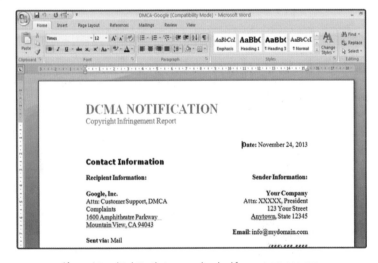

Above: A template letter that you can download from numerous sources on the internet to insist a service provider removes copyrighted work.

Hot Tip

The Digital Millennium Copyright Act (DMCA) now makes it easier to have copyrighted material removed from websites in the USA. When you report the breach to the relevant internet service, they have to issue a takedown notice.

THINKING LIKE A PUBLISHER

Being a self-published author means that you have to do much more than just write. As you need to do many of the same things that a traditional publisher does, you will have to learn to think like one.

THE ROLE OF THE PUBLISHER

Publishers do far more than just print and distribute books. They handle all aspects of book production, from editing and formatting to promotion and handling income and expenditure. In order to make a success of self-publishing, you really need to treat publishing your books as a business rather than just a hobby.

BUSINESS PLANNING

All businesses require planning. When publishers launch books to market, they do so with the expectation of getting a return on their investment. Sometimes, publishers think in the long term and, knowing that the first one or two books produced by an author may not sell well, they plan for higher returns with subsequent books. The same should be true of the self-publisher. Think in the long term and make a business plan.

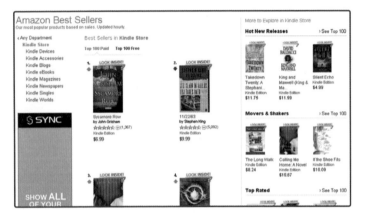

Above: The Amazon bestseller list is good for researching what's hot on the market.

Research the Market

Whatever genre you choose to write in, you need to establish the size of your potential audience. Different genres attract different numbers of readers, but these figures can change yearly, as what is hot now may not necessarily be so successful after 12 months. Publishers spend a lot of time researching the book market, identifying trends and predicting what types of books will sell well in the future.

Plan Ahead

As with all businesses, you need to think about the future. Self-publishing your first novel may require an initial outlay for editing, cover design and other production costs. You may not get a return on this investment at first, but as you produce more books, you may find that the sales of your previous titles also increase and your initial investment starts paying off.

Hot Tip

Things change quickly in publishing, so do not try to write specific types of books just because they are popular now. Look to the long term and see what sorts of things you enjoy writing which may prove popular with readers in the future.

Business Type

As a self-published author, you are self-employed. In most instances, this means that you are a sole trader, responsible for paying your taxes on any profits and for all your own expenditure. However, you could structure your business to become a company by registering it as a Limited Company (Ltd) in the UK or Limited Liability Company (LLC) in the USA.

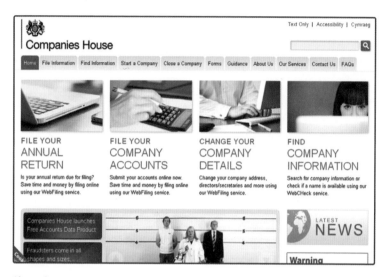

Above: Companies House in the UK allows you to set up a Limited Company.

Becoming a Publisher

Whether you remain a sole trader or become a Limited Company, you may decide to come up with a name for your business other than your own. Essentially, this means that you are becoming a small publishing house. Therefore, it may be worthwhile setting up a website under the business name, where you can advertise and sell your books. You may even decide you want to publish other people's works in the future.

> ### Hot Tip
> You do not need a business bank account to self-publish, but it can help to separate your personal and business finances, especially when it comes to paying taxes.

INCOME AND EXPENDITURE

As with any business, in order to make a profit with publishing, you need to know how much money is coming in compared to what is going out. With self-publishing, expenditure comes in two forms:

○ **Fixed costs**: The things you need to write and publish your work. Self-publishing has few fixed costs, but you may want to make a note of such things as the price of your internet connection or the cost of the computer you use for writing.

○ **Variable costs**: In self-publishing, these costs will depend on how much you are doing yourself and may include editing, formatting, cover design, etc.

Costs in Time

Even if you are making money by self-publishing, it is a good idea to put this income into context so you can judge your success. Calculate how much

Hot Tip

Working out your hourly rate for writing and publishing can make any future decision about writing full time easier.

you have earned against how much time you have put into writing, producing, distributing and marketing your book, in order to put any income into perspective.

Profit and Revenue

The money you make from sales of your books is revenue, but it is not all profit. Profit is your revenue minus your expenditure, and it is taxable. Keep a record of all your income and expenditure, and at the end of the financial year, calculate your profit.

Future Projections

All businesses make forecasts, as this helps to make future decisions. When you start selling books, track your monthly sales and make predictions, as this will help you to ascertain the success of future titles and to know whether your author platform is growing.

PRODUCTION SCHEDULING

Although self-publishing gives you the freedom to write and publish in your own time, having a production schedule can help you to be more productive and make planning much easier. Split up the different aspects of publishing and work out how long each process takes. This can help you to estimate the number of books you will be able to produce in the future.

	A	B	C	D
		Production Schedule		
		Completion Date	Duration	
	Manuscript	1/10/2014	16 weeks	
	Editing	2/10/2013	4 weeks	
	Cover	2/10/2013	4 weeks	
	Formatting	2/21/2013	2 weeks	
	Conversion	2/28/2013	1 week	
	Distribution	3/15/2013	2 weeks	

Right: Set up a production schedule to help you plan.

TAXES

The rule for registering for tax varies from country to country. You may only have to register when you file your tax returns, but in some countries, such as the UK, you have to register as soon as you start trading. Whatever the case, at the end of each financial year, you will have to send in your tax return and pay any money you owe.

IRS Withholding

The Internal Revenue Service (IRS) withholds tax for non-residents trading in the USA. This means that if you sell through an e-book retailer, such as Amazon, they will send 30 per cent of your royalties straight to the IRS. However, you can apply for a US tax number to prevent this.

Step 1: Visit the IRS website to find their contact details.

1. Contact the IRS over the phone to register your business. Their number is on their website: www.irs.gov.

2. The IRS will ask you various questions about your business and then give you an Employer Identification Number (EIN).

3. Download a W-8BEN form from the IRS website or from your e-book distributor.

4. Fill in the form, include your EIN and then post it to your e-book retailer.

VIRTUAL SHELF SPACE

When it comes to generating sales and acquiring new readers, visibility is everything. Having as many titles out on as many platforms as possible maximizes your chances of being discovered.

INFINITE SHELF SPACE

When you self-publish your first book, few people will have heard of you. Of course, your efforts at promotion should ensure a few early sales, but the majority of your readers are going to be people who discover your book while browsing online retailers. Before e-books and online bookstores, discoverability posed a problem for publishers, as bookstores only had a limited amount of space on their shelves and, therefore, could only fit in a certain number of titles. However, with online e-book stores, shelf space is unlimited.

Browsing

Online bookstores provide readers with various different ways to browse e-books. Whether a customer uses categories and subcategories, search engines or recommendations, having numerous titles on display on the virtual shelves increases your chances of people discovering your books. And once a reader has bought one and enjoyed it, there is a good chance that they will buy another.

Above: The more books you have for sale, the more likely you will be discovered.

EXTENDING YOUR REACH

In order to maximize your virtual shelf space, you need to produce new titles. Of course, writing novels takes time, but they are not your only option for increasing your body of work:

- **Short stories:** Writing short stories of 3,000–5,000 words is one way of increasing your visibility in a short space of time.

- **Novellas:** Stories between 20,000–50,000 words sell almost as well as full-length novels.

- **Novelettes:** Longer than short stories but shorter than novellas.

WRITING SHORT FICTION

Although shorter works are a good way of increasing your visibility, short stories and novelettes rarely sell as well as full-length novels or novellas. In addition, you will not be able to price your shorter works as high as your novels, which means that you may only qualify for the lower royalty rates offered by e-book retailers. However, there is a way to maximize the return on your shorter works.

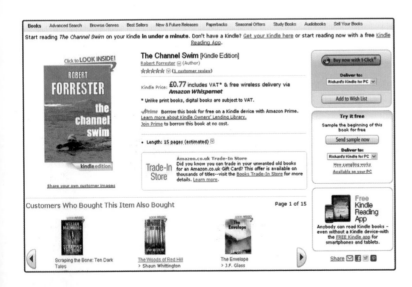

Short Story Markets

A good way of maximizing the market potential of your short stories is to try to sell them to short story

Left: Short stories will be priced lower. This book is 15 pages long and priced at £0.79.

markets before you publish them. All sorts of magazines, anthologies and e-zines pay to publish original short stories. However, you have to offer short story markets 'first rights'. This means that you cannot publish your story until after it has appeared in the magazine and often not until six to 12 months afterwards. However, after this period, you are free to self-publish the title, thus maximizing your income from the work.

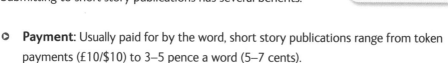

Hot Tip

If you release shorter fiction, make sure that you make it clear in the product description, in order to avoid frustrating readers who expected it to be a longer piece of work.

Submission Benefits

Submitting to short story publications has several benefits:

- **Payment**: Usually paid for by the word, short story publications range from token payments (£10/$10) to 3–5 pence a word (5–7 cents).

- **Exposure**: You get to reach a wide audience of fiction readers, some of whom may go on to buy your novels.

- **Profile**: Acceptance to some short story publications qualifies for membership to professional writers' organizations, such as SFWA (Science Fiction & Fantasy Writers of America).

Finding Short Story Markets

There are hundreds of different markets for short stories, including long-standing publications such as

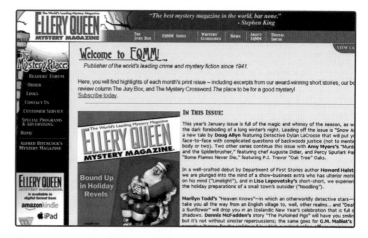

Above: There are various publications dedicated to publishing short fiction, such as *Ellery Queen's Mystery Magazine*.

Ellery Queen's Mystery Magazine, *The New Yorker*, and *Asimov's Science Fiction*. Most short-story magazines accept manuscripts by email or use online submission systems. However, make sure that you read the guidelines for each publication to ensure that you have correctly formatted your manuscript. In order to find suitable markets, several resources are available to help:

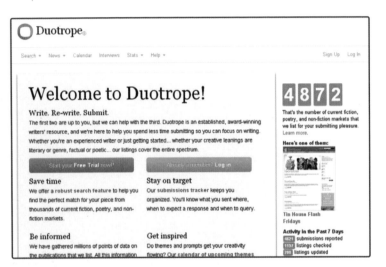

Above: Duotrope.com is a good resource for finding short story markets.

- **Writers' and Artists' Yearbook**: An annual publication that includes listings for short story markets, along with book publishers, newspapers and literary agents.

- **Duotrope.com**: An online resource that lets you search by short story genre; it requires a monthly subscription.

- **The Grinder**: A free resource available at http://thegrinder.diabolicalplots.com that lists short-story markets.

Hot Tip

When submitting to short-story markets, start with the professional publications and work your way down to the lower-paying markets, but make sure that you abide by any simultaneous-submission rules, which may insist that you do not send the same work to more than one publisher at a time.

STORY COLLECTIONS

After you have written and self-published a number of short stories, you can assemble them into a short story collection. This means that you will have another novella or novel-length work for sale, which you can sell at a higher rate than individual short stories, and also adds one more title to your body of work, thus increasing your visibility.

Serials

Splitting up a longer work into a serial is another way of increasing your virtual shelf space, although not all stories are suitable for serialization, as you need natural breaks and cliffhangers in the plot to encourage readers to buy the next instalment.

Series Writing

Readers like to buy known quantities. This is why many

Above: Bestselling author Lee Child has written several books in the Jack Reacher series.

authors choose to write books in a series: they tend to sell better than individual titles, as readers who enjoyed the first book are more likely to read the next. A series is also fun to write, as it lets you spend time with the same characters and introduce them to new situations.

PLATFORM VISIBILITY

Increasing the number of works you have available is only one way to maximize your virtual shelf space. Another way is to ensure that your titles are available in as many e-book platforms as possible. While you may have to use an aggregator service such as Smashwords to reach some platforms, if you have six or seven titles out, including novels, novellas and short stories, as well as print editions, you have more chance of people discovering them if they are listed everywhere rather than just in one or two markets.

Cross-selling

Since the greatest advertisements for increasing your readers are the books you have for sale, make sure that you include descriptions at the back of each title for all your other work.

By the Same Author
Murder Laid Bare

When a body is discovered on a nudist beach, the struggling seaside resort of Milhaven is thrust into the media spotlight. Fortunately, Inspector Hope has just arrived at the sleepy coastal town, much to the annoyance of brassy Detective Sergeant Elaine Carver.

Forced to work together, the temperamental Carver and rather prudish Hope delve into the dead man's past and uncover a darker side to the goings on at the seemingly innocent nudist resort. Both Hope and Carver are themselves hiding dark secrets and have far more in common than they think. The investigation soon leads them on a path of self-discovery where they have to face their inner demons as they uncover the seedier side to middle class suburbia.

Available as an eBook from Amazon US/UK

Hot Tip

Every time you release a new title, resubmit all your other work with a description and link to your latest book at the back.

Left: At the back of your book, mention your other works, as well as links to where they can be bought.

COPING WITH SUCCESS

When your books start selling, you will have to face many of the uncertainties of publishing, such as criticism, fluctuating sales and even a demand to write more books – and coping with all of this can be difficult.

WRITING AS A PROFESSION

Whether you are selling hundreds of books each week and generating a full-time wage or only selling a handful of copies and making a little extra money to supplement your income, you need to regard writing as a profession and not do anything that will damage your author platform.

Maintain Quality

Make sure that your books are always put together as professionally as possible. If readers complain after spotting typographical errors or formatting issues, make sure that you correct these as soon as possible and reissue an amended version.

Hot Tip

If somebody leaves a bad review due to errors in your work, reissue it and mention in the product description that previous issues have been addressed.

CRITICISM

One aspect of selling books online that is different from high-street retailing is the ability for customers to leave reviews. Customer reviews are there to help other people with their buying decisions, so it makes sense that a book with a high number of positive reviews will sell more copies.

Lack of Customer Reviews

Not all your readers will leave a review. In fact, you can sell hundreds of copies of a book before somebody provides any feedback, which is why many authors opt to solicit reviews from readers. However, this is not without its problems:

- **Bias**: Reviews from people you know or those you have paid for are against the guidelines on most online stores.

Left: Amazon reviewers are themselves gauged for quality.

- **Quality:** Amazon's reviewers are given a quality score based on customer feedback, which many people use to gauge the usefulness of reviews.

- **Negative reviews:** Not everyone will like your book, and the more reviews you solicit, the more likely you will be to receive negative comments.

Finding Reviewers

If you do wish to seek reviewers, you need to approach people who will give an unbiased, quality review, as well as finding those readers who are more likely to enjoy you book.

1. Search for titles in a genre similar to that of your book on Amazon or another online e-book retailer.

2. View the customer reviews and click on the individual reviewers.

3. See what other types of books the reviewers enjoyed.

4. Click on the profile of the reviewers and check their review score (if they have one).

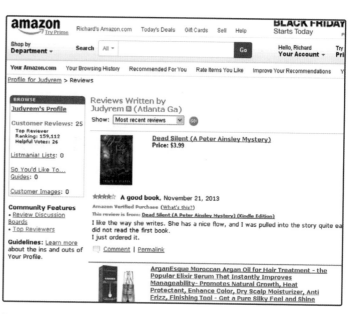

Step 4: Visit reviewers' profiles and look at their stats.

5. If the reviewer has an email address listed, contact them and ask if they would consider reviewing your book.

Negative Criticism

Not everybody will like your work, and some people may perhaps hate it, but do not take their comments personally. Even bestsellers and classic titles acquire a number of negative reviews. Take on board any constructive criticism, but refrain from responding to negative feedback.

> **Hot Tip**
> Never try to buy reviews or bribe a reviewer. Always allow people free rein to leave either positive or negative comments.

FLUCTUATING SALES

Sales fluctuate, and just because your e-book has started to sell a certain number of copies each week, it does not mean that it will continue to do so. For some people, e-book sales start slow and then gradually build momentum as they develop their author platform. For others, e-book sales may start with a surge and then decline rapidly.

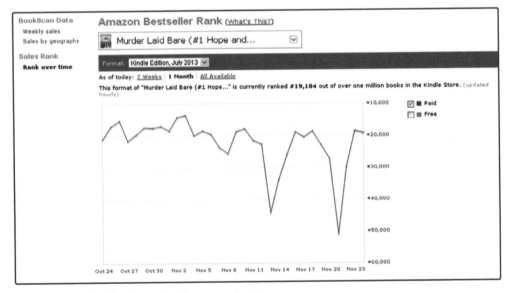

Above: The sales rank graph on Amazon shows how sales can fluctuate.

Individual Title Sales

Not only do overall sales fluctuate, but also the sales of different titles vary, even those in a series. Just because one book sold well, it does not necessarily mean that the next in the series will sell as many. Of course, the reverse may be true, and the second book in a series could outsell the first – you can never tell.

Write, Publish, Sell

Sales are generally out of a writer's control. The best way to improve sales and boost your author platform over time is to continue to write and publish titles to the best of your ability, thus carrying on any momentum generated by your previous sales.

MARKET DEMANDS

When you start selling your work and receive a modicum of success, you may find that certain types of books are outselling others. This may mean that you have to decide on the direction in which you want to take your career:

Above: Arthur Conan Doyle famously grew to hate writing Sherlock Holmes books and tried to kill him off.

- **Write what sells:** You choose to write what sells the best. This means that you are letting the market control your creative output.

- **Write what you enjoy:** You continue to produce books that you enjoy writing and hope that they become successful.

Creative Compromise

The last thing any writer wants is for it to become a chore. If you are writing strictly to meet the demands

---

Hot Tip

Some writers write one book for the market and one for themselves, while others try to tailor their work to include elements that satisfy both the author and the reader.

of the market, you may fall out of love with your characters and ideas. In addition, if you are writing solely what you want, without thinking about your readers, you may find that your books stop selling.

Meeting Demand

When your books start selling, readers may begin to ask when the next one is due for release. While this can be flattering, writing books to meet demand and to keep building your author platform brings its own problems:

○ **Time**: You may need to dedicate more time to writing and publishing. This could mean restructuring your life, such as going part-time in your day job or even giving it up to write full time.

- **Inspiration**: You will need to come up with more new story ideas, plots and characters.

- **Business**: The more books you have for sale, the more time and effort you will have to put into the business of publishing.

Taking the Plunge

Many authors hold the ambition that one day they will earn enough to give up work and write full time. Self-publishing has allowed an ever-increasing number of writers to achieve this dream. Knowing when the time is right to become a full-time author will depend on your required income and personal circumstances.

> **Hot Tip**
>
> If you are thinking of becoming a full-time author, make sure that you have enough savings to cover your bills if things do not work out as well as you hoped to begin with.

AUTHOR COMMUNITY

Being an author means that you are part of a larger community. You should not think of other writers as competitors but as a way to introduce more people to your books. For instance, if a reader who has never bought a book in a particular genre chooses to buy one from another author and enjoys it, then they may decide to buy one of your books in the future.

Collaboration and Interaction

Interacting with other authors is a great way to improve your writing. In addition, you could find

Above: Kindle Boards is a popular writers' forum, especially for self-published authors.

writers who may wish to collaborate on a project with you. This is a great way to share your readership, increase your individual author platform and boost your visibility.

Helping Others Succeed

Self-publishing has a steep learning curve, involving a lot of experiment and trial and error. If you have achieved some degree of success, it can often be gratifying to help other authors by offering advice on writing forums and websites, and sharing what you have learned. You may even wish to begin your own writing blog or online workshop, where you can assist other writers and share your knowledge.

The Publishing/Self-publishing Divide

One unsavoury aspect of writing that has emerged with the rise of self-publishing is the divide between some self-published authors and some of those who operate in the traditional publishing sphere. Numerous websites and forums have emerged where the majority takes either one side or the other. Some of the people who comment on these platforms can be quite vocal when discussing different aspects of publishing, which has led to a number of authors feeling bullied or harangued when they comment or seek advice. It is best to avoid websites that have an unhealthy bias towards one type of publishing over the other.

PUBLISHING OPTIONS

Once you have a proven track record, or some of your books have entered various bestseller lists, you may find that publishers and literary agents start to approach you. Signing up with a traditional publisher can bring with it many rewards, such as expanded distribution, seeing your books in high street bookstores, and having the support of an editor and publishing house behind you. However, it also has its downsides, so make sure that you know what you are getting into before you sign away the rights to your books.

- **Royalties**: Make sure that you know how much money you will be receiving in both royalties and advances. Calculate this against what you are currently earning by self-publishing.

- **Rights**: Make sure that you know what rights you are giving away, such as print-only or e-book and print. Also, make sure that you know for how long the publisher will own the rights.

- **Competition clauses**: Some publishing contracts include non-compete clauses, which may stop you writing and publishing any more books in the same genre.

Publishing Contract

ıblishers exclusive world-wide electronic and print
! for all renewals and extensions of copyright. This

gital formats including all online formats carried

BOUTIQUE SELF-PUBLISHING HOUSES

Although self-publishing provides authors with a platform to write and distribute their books, it does require a lot of work. However, for those authors who just want to write but do not want to go through the traditional publishing route, there is a third way.

SELF-PUBLISHING HOUSES

The rise of self-publishing has allowed writers to publish and distribute their own work, but also it has made it easier for people to start their own small publishing houses to publish the work of others. Many of these operate in the traditional publishing model. However, an increasing number have become a type of hybrid publisher, operating somewhere between the self-publishing and traditional publishing models.

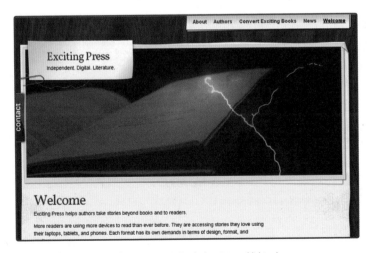

Above: Exciting Press is an example of a boutique publishing house.

- **Traditional publishing:** You sign the rights to your book to a publisher, who handles all the editing, production and distribution and pays you royalties on book sales.

- **Self-publishing:** You retain all the rights and royalties, but you have to handle all the production and distribution yourself.

- ○ **Boutique publishing**: You retain all the rights, but the publisher handles the editing, production and distribution, and you pay them a royalty on each sale.

Royalties and Rights

With these new boutique publishing houses, the author usually retains his or her rights. This is in contrast to the traditional model, where writers normally sign print and/or e-book rights over to the publisher. In addition, rather than the publisher paying the author a royalty (normally around 8–12 per cent in traditional publishing), with boutique publishing, it is the other way around, with the publisher getting a royalty of between 10–15 per cent for each book sold.

Production

The big benefit that boutique publishing offers authors is that they handle all aspects of production, from editing and formatting to distribution, meaning that writers do not have to pay for these services. Boutique publishers often offer some limited promotional assistance too, as it is in their best interest to sell more books.

Above: Writer Beware is a good website for establishing which publishers are good and which are bad.

Hot Tip

Never pay money upfront to any publisher, no matter what they say it is for. Upfront fees are normally a sign of vanity publishing.

Submissions

The big downside to boutique publishing is that they can only produce a limited number of books, so authors have to submit books for consideration just as is the case for the traditional model.

Some Boutique Publishers

Above: A/A Productions specializes in the horror, fantasy, science fiction and mystery genres.

- **A/A Productions (www. aaprod.weebly.com)**: Specializes in dark fantasy and crime. The publisher takes 15 per cent of all royalties, while the rest goes to the author.

- **Excitingpress.com**: Publishes novels, novellas and short stories, and distributes them to major online retailers.

Agent-assisted Self-publishing

Literary agents are also now offering similar services to boutique publishers. The agent arranges editing and formatting before uploading the author's file to self-publishing platforms and then takes a 15 per cent fee on all royalties. Agent-assisted publishing is more common for traditionally published authors who have failed to sell a book or who want to retain more control over their next work. Few agents will be willing to sign up an unknown author and offer assisted self-publishing services.

VANITY PUBLISHING

Vanity publishing has a bad reputation, and quite rightly so. Vanity publishers have been around for as long as there have been authors and publishers. In short, they are those that charge a fee – paid in advance by the author – for all aspects of book production, such as editing, formatting and distribution.

Costs

The services offered by vanity publishers can be extremely expensive, with some authors having to invest thousands of pounds/dollars before being able to bring their book to market. Some vanity publishers even secure rights, meaning that they have full control of the work and can take royalties for every sale. Few authors who pay for vanity publishing ever get a return on their investment.

OTHER PUBLISHING OPTIONS

Some traditional publishers are providing platforms where authors can upload their work and bring it to the attention of readers, thus enabling the publisher to find popular works that are worth investing in. One such project, authonomy (www.authonomy.com), is run by HarperCollins.

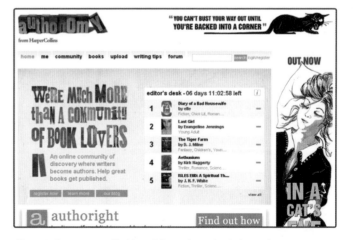

Above: Authonomy, owned by HarperCollins, is designed to find new talent.

FURTHER READING

Brewer, Robert L., *2014 Guide to Self-Publishing*, Writer's Digest Books, 2013.

Gallacher, Seumas, *Self-Publishing Steps To Successful Sales*, SGC Publishing, 2014.

Hitz, Shelley, *Self Publishing Books 101: Helping You Get Published and Noticed*, CreateSpace Independent Publishing Platform, 2012.

Kawasaki, Guy and Welch, Shawn, *APE: Author, Publisher, Entrepeneur – How to Publish a Book*, Nononina Press, 2013.

King, Carla, *How to Self-Publish Your Books: A practical guide to creating and distributing your e-book or print book*, Public Broadcasting Service, 2013.

Levine, Mark, *The Fine Print of Self-Publishing, Fifth Edition: A Primer on Contracts, Printing Costs, Royalties, Distribution, E-Books, and Marketing*, Bascon Hill Publishing Group, 2014.

Poynter, Dan, *Dan Poynter's Self-Publishing Manual: How to Write, Print and Sell Your Own Book*, Para Publishing, 2007.

Verma, Shiv, *Book Authority: How to Write, Self-Publish & Market Your Book*, Vital Acts Inc., 2014.

USEFUL WEBSITES

www.alanrinzler.com/blog
Alan Rinzler is a consulting editor whose blog offers advice on the many aspects of self-publishing.

authorcentral.amazon.com
Amazon Author Central is a site that allows independent authors to market and sell their books.

www.authorbuzz.com
AuthorBuzz is a marketing service that puts authors directly in touch with readers, reading groups, booksellers and librarians.

www.authorhouse.com
AuthorHouse is a top self-publishing firm that provides services to authors around the world, with over 60,000 titles released.

www.blueink.com
BlueInk Review reviews self-published books, as well as vigorously promoting certain titles to publishers, librarians and literary agents and editors.

www.createspace.com
A website that makes it simple to distribute your books through internet retail outlets, your own website, and other bookstores, retailers, libraries and academic institutions.

www.thecreativepenn.com/publishing
The Creative Penn is a resource offering all sorts of information and articles on the topic of self-publishing.

www.goodreads.com
Goodreads is a social media platform based around books and authors.

www.ingramcontent.com
A comprehensive publishing industry services company that offers numerous solutions, including physical book distribution, print-on-demand and digital services.

www.iuniverse.com
iUniverse provides an alternative to traditional publishing. It offers a wide range of self-publishing services and publishes books professionally and affordably.

www.kirkusreviews.com
Kirkus Reviews is an authoritative book-reviewing firm in the book industry.

kpd.amazon.com
On Kindle Direct Publishing, publish your books independently on the Amazon Kindle Store, where it will be available on Amazon websites globally and reach a very large audience.

www.lightningsource.com
Lightning Source is a print on demand publisher which distributes books to all retailers, libraries and academic institutions.

www.lulu.com/publishing
A leading independent self-publishing company that publishes books to just about anywhere, including print, e-readers and tablet devices.

www.narcissus.me/blog
A blog that provides information and advice about self-publishing.

www.outskirtspress.com
Outskirtspress is a full-service book-publishing and book-marketing firm. The company helps authors write, publish and market their books.

www.publishersweekly.com
Publishers Weekly publishes *PW Select*, a monthly supplement dedicated to covering the self-publishing industry.

www.selfpublishing.com
This website helps authors become publishers with in-depth information on the multifaceted nature of publishing.

www.smashwords.com
Smashwords is the world's largest distributor of indie e-books, publishing and distributing e-books to major retailers.

www.xlibris.com
Xlibris is one of the pioneering self-publishing companies that believe that authors should have control over their work.

INDEX